D1130681

Michael Drayton

and the Passing of Elizabethan England

Michael Drayton

By permission of Dulwich College Picture Gallery

Michael Drayton
and
the Passing
of
Elizabethan England

by
Richard F. Hardin

THE UNIVERSITY PRESS OF KANSAS
Lawrence/Manhattan/Wichita

© Copyright 1973 by The University Press of Kansas
Standard Book Number 7006-0103-1
Library of Congress Catalog Card Number 72-93752
Printed in the United States of America

Designed by Fritz Reiber

Preface

If the annual scholarly bibliographies are any indication, Michael Drayton is today the least fashionable of important Elizabethan poets. Those who know his poems recognize that the best of them deserve the attention of any literate reader, and that historians of the Jacobean age can learn from the social criticism that they contain. Yet neither literary historians nor social historians seem especially informed about his work today, the tendency being to shunt him off with Daniel, Campion, and "others" as one more star in a galaxy of able performers. We are either shocked or amused to find that our great-grandfathers allotted him an entire chapter in *The Cambridge History of English Literature*.

His eclipse came with the "rediscovery" of Donne and the Metaphysicals in the decades just after the publication of the *Cambridge History*, when an increasing number of important critics began to view Drayton, "the Petrarchans," and even Spenser as so many pedantic weeds in the Muse's garden *ante Donne*. Eliot observed in "Imperfect Critics" that the only good lines in Drayton's "dreary sequence of ideas" occur when he "drops his costume for a moment and talks in terms of actuality." Yvor Winters, in his notable revaluation of Elizabethan poetry, placed Drayton among the rhetorically obsessed, morally unenlightening family of Petrarchans. Followers of Eliot and Winters—through devotion to their masters, one feels, rather than first-hand acquaintance with Drayton's poetry—have perpetuated the view of Drayton as a tedious Petrarchan or a tiresome drudge. It is a view that still prevails in many quarters, notwithstanding the respect for Drayton evinced in such important studies as Rosemond Tuve's *Elizabethan and Metaphysical Imagery* and Hallett Smith's *Elizabethan Poetry*.

Drayton was surely a different kind of poet from Donne, and the sort of poetry for which Drayton was most applauded in his time, historical poetry, has little if any audience today, in contrast to the intensely personal, apolitical poetry of Donne. Donne's first audience, like his audience today, was an urbanized one: London professional men, intellectuals, members of the Establishment. Drayton wrote for a more geographically dispersed audience of country gentlemen and lesser aristocrats sharing his conservative political, religious, and intellectual outlook. Donne's poetry, except for a few occasional pieces, was written for the private enjoyment of a sophisticated coterie delighting in his mastery of wit, surprise, and conceit. Drayton, like Spenser, was a public poet moved by an educated faith in English destiny—truly "Elizabethan," as historians have come to understand that term, in his persistent desire to raise English poetry and national fame above that of other cultures, past and present.

My purpose in this essay is not to restore Drayton to the place of eminence he held in his time—no one can do that; rather, it is to impart a sense of his identity as a poet, particularly to explain how he is distinguished among his contemporaries by the intensity of his devotion to England and English traditions. In making a case for Drayton's consistency as a patriot, I confess to an interest in his sincerity. Admittedly a sincere patriot has no more right to Parnassus than a sincere butcher; it might even be argued that sincerity among poets is a vice, like compassion in first sergeants. Nevertheless, sincerity is an important dimension of a man's personality and therefore of what he writes, and in this book I have set out more to understand Drayton than to evaluate his poems. I hope there are still readers who are interested in poets as well as poems.

The aim of my first chapter is to set Drayton apart from his fellow poets in the school of the 1590s, and to show how he evolved from an imitator into a poet of essentially unique temperament and concerns. The next four chapters concentrate on the two areas in which Drayton's patriotism is best examined, his historical poetry and satire. The last chapter is an extension of these, underlining Drayton's vision of England's future and his final verdict on her present, as given a decade before the outbreak of the Civil War. If in the process I convince a few critics, historians, or common readers that Drayton is worth their time, I shall not consider my work in vain.

I am especially in debt to J. William Hebel, Kathleen Tillotson, B. H. Newdigate, and B. E. Juel-Jensen for their splendid edition, *The Works of Michael Drayton* (5 vols., Oxford: B. Blackwell, 1931–41; corrected edition, 1961), and to Mr. Newdigate again for his *Michael Drayton and His Circle* (Oxford: B. Blackwell, 1941; corrected edition, 1961). In footnotes I refer to these as *"Works"* and "Newdigate," respectively. I use the text of the Hebel edition throughout; however, I have modernized the spelling of the text, as of all old-spelling texts, when quoting, except when prosody requires the original. Several scholarly works stimulated my thinking on Drayton and his age, especially P. G. Buchloh's study of *Poly-Olbion*, entitled *Michael Drayton, Barde und Historiker, Politiker und Prophet*, Raymond Jenkins' "Drayton's Relation to the School of Donne," and Lawrence Stone's monumental *Crisis of the Aristocracy*. Regrettably, Joan Grundy's full and stimulating treatment of Drayton in *The Spenserian Poets* came to my attention only after I had completed this study.

I owe a more personal acknowledgment to several accomplished scholar-teachers: Professors Robert Montgomery, Alexander Sackton, James Sledd, and especially Thomas Harrison, through whom I first came to know Drayton's poetry. In addition, valuable advice or assistance was given by Mr. W. W. S. Breem, Librarian of the Inner Temple, Mr. J. P. Brooke-Little of the College of Arms, Professor Sears Jayne of Brown University, Dr. B. E. Juel-Jensen, and Mr. Daniel Patterson. I wish to thank the Research Council of the University of Kansas for a generous grant in support of this study, and my colleagues at Kansas, Peter Casagrande and William Scott, for their helpful comments on the manuscript while it was undergoing revision.

Contents

Michael Drayton:
Chronology

(A complete list of Drayton's writings, with dates of publication, will be found in the index.)

1563   Born at Hartshill, near Atherstone, in Warwickshire.

1573   Page in the household of Henry Goodere, probably remaining with Gooderes until manhood.

1591   Publishes first poetry, *The Harmony of the Church*.

1597–1602 Playwright for Philip Henslowe.

1603   Sir Walter Aston is made Knight of the Bath, with Drayton as his Esquire.

1608   With several others, takes over management of the Whitefriars Playhouse and the Children of the King's Revels. The venture fails before the year is out.

1612   Receives a small bequest from Henry Prince of Wales, to whom he dedicates the first part of *Poly-Olbion*.

1616   Supposed to have taken part in a "merry meeting" with Shakespeare and Jonson, shortly before Shakespeare's death.

1618   Begins occasional correspondence with William Drummond.

1630   Publishes last poetry, *The Muses' Elysium*, with *Divine Poems*.

1631   Dies c. 23 December at London, buried in Westminster Abbey.

1 | PRELIMINARIES

My native country, then, which so brave spirits hast bred,
If there be virtue yet remaining in thy earth,
Or any good of thine thou breathd'st into my birth,
Accept it as thine own whilst now I sing of thee;
Of all thy later brood, unworthiest though I be.

(Poly-Olbion XIII.8–12)

The Essential Drayton

The standard edition of Michael Drayton's works contains about two thousand pages of verse in four volumes. Even when we take into account the many revised poems, which comprise a large part of one volume, we are still left with a formidable amount of poetry. Add to this the scant critical attention that has been paid Drayton, and one hardly knows how to approach him. He wrote sonnets and other brief lyric poems, but he wrote the enormous *Poly-Olbion* as well, not to mention several long historical pieces. He attempted almost all the kinds of poetry known in his day, and did well in most of them: religious, heroic, pastoral, elegiac, and satiric. He had a hand in writing a number of plays, and he introduced two "new" kinds of poetry into England with his heroic epistles and odes.

From this wide range of poetry, the reader who wants a few poems containing the essence of Drayton should, I believe, choose the odes, first published in 1606, later augmented in the collected *Poems* of 1619. If need be, he can narrow the essential list still

1

further to four odes, the first two of which are his best: "To the Virginian Voyage," "Ballad of Agincourt," "An Ode Written in the Peak," and "A Hymn to His Lady's Birthplace." (For the reader's convenience, these poems are reprinted in Appendix A.)

Short as they are, these few poems exemplify the Drayton of the long historical and topographical works: the public poet who employed his talent for the celebration of his country; the conservative spokesman for the traditions and values of rural English gentlemen; the Elizabethan imbued with a sense of his country's destiny. In each of them, the object of praise is not so much the lady or the heroes of Agincourt and Virginia as it is England herself—the England who is chief actor and principal object of praise in *Poly-Olbion*. As in nearly all Drayton's poems, there is in these a fundamental, radical Englishness, for their author was the most English poet of his age, if not of all others. At a later date his kind of patriotism in poets can often be attributed to simple-mindedness or crass hypocrisy, but in the early 1600s the current of nationalism in England was still fresh enough that a bit of her landscape or history could produce deep and powerful sentiments in the audience. For this reason, in discussing the four poems that I have chosen as representative—and in treating the rest of Drayton's poetry, for that matter—I often disregard the distinction usually made between the poet and the persona speaking in his poems. For the most part the two voices are virtually one and the same, as I believe they must be in the poetry of celebration.

"An Ode Written in the Peak" reflects Drayton's awareness of the classical tradition of the ode: like Martial's epigram on the villa of Faustinus at Baiae, or Horace's poems on his Sabine farm, it is a poem in praise of a place. But the difference between Drayton and his Roman antecedents is important, for they had written on a place belonging to someone, while Drayton wrote on a place that belonged to all England. As the earlier poets had associated the virtues of the place with its owner, Drayton extols the English virtues of the Peak; thus the contrast on which his poem is built, between the cold North and warm South, extends beyond England to the greater rivalry between the civilizations of southern and northern Europe.

The mood is one of celebration, but lightly recreative, like many passages elsewhere in Drayton. He begins by wondering whether any poet can work "Exposed to sleet and rain" in the wintery Peak:

> This while we are abroad,
> Shall we not touch our lyre?
> Shall we not sing an ode?
> Shall that holy fire,
> In us that strongly glowed,
> In this cold air expire?

As we should expect of the author of *Poly-Olbion*, he cannot avoid pointing out the local tourist attractions, the clear rivers and the caves, but most of all those two sovereign emblems of English gemütlichkeit, "Buckston's delicious baths," topped off with "Strong ale and noble cheer,/T'assuage breme Winter's scathes." The poem concludes on a pun: wherever the place, at whatever time, "The Muse is still in ure"—playing on the Latin sense (*uro*, "burn") to suggest that the holy fire of the opening stanza is always alive. Poetry does not thrive in one particular place and time, just as the poetry of the Northern culture can compete with that of the Mediterranean South, whether ancient or modern. National competition is a familiar theme in Drayton, perhaps most fully explored by Surrey and Geraldine in *England's Heroical Epistles*.

Another representative ode, "A Hymn to His Lady's Birthplace" (first printed in 1619), shows how the poem in praise of a person can be manipulated by Drayton into the kind of patriotic tribute he enjoyed writing. This expression of esteem for the daughter of his old patron might, for another poet, have been the occasion for a more intimate poem, but the "Hymn" is every bit as public as the other three odes. Like Spenser's *Prothalamion*, it shows a divided concern for the subject of his praise and the places with which she is associated, as if these places have a life and personality of their own. Coventry is elevated to a national shrine honoring Idea's (Anne Goodere's) birthplace, and as in the "Ode Written in the Peak" Drayton celebrates the local attributes (the city prospect, its walls and spires, the "trophies of the boar") but generalizes upon their patriotic implications.

Far superior to either of these as a patriotic poem is the ode "To the Virginian Voyage," entered for publication when the patent for the Virginia colony was less than two weeks old. Behind this singular poem are two important influences—first, Richard Hakluyt, a favorite mine of information for Drayton and a guiding spirit behind his poetry. Hakluyt and he had much in common: both were country gentlemen in origin, both sought to make Englishmen aware of their national superiority through patient, sometimes plodding historical research. And if ever the first propagandist for English imperialism found a disciple it was Drayton. "Industrious Hakluyt," he calls him in the ode:

> Whose reading shall inflame
> Men to seek fame,
> And much commend
> To after-times thy wit.

Privately, Drayton must have wished the same for his own writings —if not in all his work, at least in this poem, one of the few great English poems of empire, drawing its strength from the very newness of that theme in the national culture.

A second influence in the poem is the ancient dream of the earthly paradise, the land of abundance and eternal spring that men had long believed lay far to the west of Europe. Columbus had been the first of many explorers to identify America with this mythical place, and in England the association had become fairly common by the seventeenth century. Some were convinced that Virginia lay on the threshold of Eden; Drayton portrays it as a natural paradise, "Earth's only paradise," where "the golden age / Still Nature's laws doth give." In a land where the profiteers had not yet enclosed the farmland and ravaged the forests—familiar topics in Drayton's later satire—Englishmen might hope to live in the same spirit of justice as had prevailed in primitive times.

Beside this return to natural justice, the earthly paradise would bring freedom from want. Drayton is lured by the same promise that had excited men like John Smith and Arthur Barlow about the new England:

> Where Nature hath in store
> Fowl, venison, and fish,
> And the fruitfull'st soil,
> Without your toil,
> Three harvests more,
> All greater than you wish.

At a later time, when Goldsmith could describe a nightmarish land across the Atlantic, where "crouching tigers wait their hapless prey, And savage men more murd'rous still than they," men might with reason dismiss this poem as naïve, infused as it was with the enthusiasm of a generation who, like Hakluyt and Drayton, never experienced the hazards of actual colonial life.

The heavy emphasis on material abundance in the ode, particularly Drayton's urging the voyagers "to get the pearl and gold," leads us to think that its author had only the material advancement of England in mind. The whole poem, however, with its promise of safe voyage and wealth, rises to one climactic stanza, the keystone of the arch. Drayton exhorts the voyagers to thank God for their success, to be happy,

> And in regions far
> Such Heroes bring ye forth,
> As those from whom we came,
> And plant our name
> Under that star
> Not known unto our North.

This Virginian voyage was not just another foraging excursion or exploratory trip, like the expeditions of the sixteenth century. If we exclude those often abortive attempts, it marks the beginning of a continued English presence in the New World. In the ode, particularly in the stanza I have just quoted, Drayton is doing nothing less than celebrating the birth of America. The voyagers are not only to enjoy their material prosperity, they are to increase and multiply: to bring forth "heroes," like the Englishmen of old whom Drayton so often celebrates in his historical poetry. Just as Nature's profusion in Virginia contrasts with her poverty in the Old World, the new race of Virginians will signal a return to the age of heroes. Drayton accepts the antiquarian paradox that the modern world is the world grown old, so that the phrase "New World" held a special significance for him. Indeed, the famous opening stanza can only be read in the light of this contrast between the heroes of the New World and the burnt-out men of the Old:

> You brave heroic minds,
> Worthy your country's name,

> That honor still pursue,
> Go, and subdue,
> Whilst loit'ring hinds
> Lurk here at home, with shame.

It is no coincidence that this and the previously quoted stanza echo the words of God to Adam: "Be fruitful and multiply, and fill the earth and subdue it." During the early seventeenth century, the idea became commonplace that English expansion was somehow a re-enactment of that which God ordained for the elect of the Old Testament, from Adam and Noah to Abraham and Moses. Many puritan New Englanders thought of themselves as righteous outcasts from a modern Egypt, seeking a new Canaan.[1]

The bulk of Drayton's writing is historical poetry, and I believe that the "Virginian Voyage," even though it looks to the future rather than the past, fits into the overall scheme of the historical work. The whole Elizabethan impulse toward colonial expansion derives from the same spirit that Drayton's work and the historical drama of the Elizabethan stage may be said to embody. The wars with France in the fifteenth century had been an earlier stage of the development of a national identity, and the resulting desire to expand this time took the form of colonial expeditions.[2] Thus there is a continuity between the spirit of the "Virginian Voyage" and the last poem in our representative list, the "Ballad of Agincourt."

Like many of his countrymen Drayton was disappointed in James I's failure to pursue an aggressive policy of colonial expansion and to assert himself militarily on the Continent as earlier English rulers had done. The ideal monarch in this respect was of course Henry V, who figures prominently in Drayton's long *Battle of Agincourt* and in the "Ballad." As is the case with all his historical verse, this poem passes judgment on the present and past, and does so in fact by holding up to contemporary Englishmen the example of their forefathers. It was probably Drayton's favorite among his own works, for in the preface to the odes he singles it out:

> [I] would at this time also gladly let thee understand, what
> I think above the rest, of the last ode of this number [i.e.,
> the "Ballad"], or if thou wilt, ballad in my book: for both
> the great master of Italian rhymes, Petrarch, and our
> Chaucer, and other of the upper house of the Muses, have

thought their canzons honored in the title of a ballad; which, for that I labor to meet truly therein with the old English garb, I hope as able to justify, as the learned Colin Clout his roundelay.

These remarks, beside showing Drayton's esteem for the poem, suggest that he called it a ballad because that kind of poetry had a venerable tradition in England, notwithstanding its abuse by contemporary hacks. Moreover, he meant the ballad to be sung: both the preface and the ensuing verse-history of the ode ("To Himself, and the Harp") show that he thought of odes as necessarily accompanied by music. As a matter of fact, he urges Sir Henry Goodere to have his harper, John Hewes, sing them.[3] This explains his dedicating the "Ballad" "To the Cambro-Britains and Their Harp."[4]

Drayton's mention of "the old English garb" in the foregoing passage implies a desire to infuse into his ode the spirit as well as the form of the medieval English war ballad. How much of this kind of poetry he knew is uncertain, but through his antiquarian friends William Camden and John Stowe he would have had access to many poems of this kind, even to early medieval specimens. The "Ballad of Agincourt" is, in fact, the closest thing to an Anglo-Saxon war poem to be written in Drayton's age. Henry's rallying speech is a virtual *bēot*, displaying the single-minded fatalism of an ancient Germanic hero; and the description of the battle itself recalls the camaraderie of "The Battle of Maldon":

> None from his fellow starts,
> But playing manly parts,
> And like true English hearts
> Stuck close together.

But in this battle there are no cowards, at least on the English side: King Henry might be called the hero of the poem, but this would be misleading, for every Englishman is valorous. The listing of names and attributes of each prominent English leader lends the ode a heroic breadth that is difficult to attain in so short a poem. Even the typography conveys a sense of sustained monumentality:

> WARWICK in blood did wade,
> OXFORD the foe invade,
> And cruel slaughter made,

> Still as they ran up;
> SUFFOLK his ax did ply,
> BEAUMONT and WILLOUGHBY
> Bare them right doughtily,
> FERRERS and FANHOPE.

Nothing in the poem mitigates this relentless martial spirit, no sense of the irony or paradox of human warfare. The prevailing tone is, on the contrary, quite heartless, as when the English archers rush the Frenchmen after firing their arrows:

> When down their bows they threw,
> And forth their bilboes drew,
> And on the French they flew,
> Not one was tardy;
> Arms were from shoulders sent,
> Scalps to the teeth were rent,
> Down the French peasants went,
> Our men were hardy.

Some may see the starkness of the poem as a fault—certainly it does not have the emotional complexity of a lyric by Donne or Shakespeare; the emotion itself, however, is not a simple one to account for in men, and I cannot think of another short poem in English that has conveyed it quite so successfully, in all its bare and terrible directness, as Drayton's ode.

The closing lines of the "Ballad" were intended to bring the seventeenth-century reader back into the present, with a thinly concealed contrast between Henry V and James I. From them we may infer that James's weaknesses were two—being a pacifist and being a Scot:

> O, when shall *English* men
> With such acts fill a pen,
> Or *England* breed again
> Such a King HARRY?

If we find the chauvinism of these lines unfortunate, it can only be said in mitigation that Drayton was not alone. Englishmen from Ascham to Milton shared his zealous patriotism, and the feeling is not exactly lacking in Shakespeare. And aside from Shakespeare there are few moments in English poetry that impart so convincingly the mood of a man convinced of his nation's destiny as "The Virginian Voyage" and the "Ballad of Agincourt."

From these four odes, then, we may abstract the motives underlying almost all of Drayton's work: the desire to place English poetry in competition with that of the ancients and moderns of other countries; to revere the past and praise the natural beauty of England; to make clear to his English readers their virtues as a people. His poems are historical, topographical, encomiastic, occasionally indignant; but they are above all English.

Apprenticeship

If we except the crude imitations of Ronsard by John Southern (*Pandora*, 1584), Drayton's are the first English odes, or more properly, the first poems so called having a legitimate claim to the name in their Horatian characteristics. Like so many of his contemporaries Drayton was as conservative in poetry as he was in his politics, yet in spite of his traditionalism he produced much that was new. Unlike other Renaissance poets, he never lost touch with the past in his new poems: if he introduced odes into English literature, he also continued writing the kinds of verse that had already been out of date in his youth. His *Cromwell* was virtually the last poem in the line of *Mirror for Magistrates* tragedies, while *Robert Duke of Normandy* is one of the last English dream-visions, enhanced by a venerable allegorical pair named Fame and Fortune.

The reason Drayton never became quite so "modern," or at least unmedieval, as Shakespeare and Spenser is perhaps to be found in his origins. He was born in rural Warwickshire in 1563, and a few years later, in the old feudal way, went to serve as a page for the family of a landed gentleman, Henry Goodere. In Goodere's country manor Drayton received all his formal education and, as he tells us in the elegy "To Henry Reynolds," formed his taste in poetry around the romances and ballads of England's past. He stayed with the family until manhood. This is wholly unlike the upbringing of Spenser, a London boy with a good grammar-school and university education. Shakespeare, too, though he hailed from Drayton's shire, grew up in dissimilar circumstances: his father was a tradesman in a thriving market town; he was educated in a grammar school, not by a tutor.

Drayton broke with his feudal surroundings in 1591 when he came to London with Goodere and published his first book, *The Harmony of the Church*, a set of verse translations of prayers from the Old Testament. From then on his work obliged him to spend much of his time in London—although the only thing he ever liked about the city was its history. Once his reputation became secure, he remained attached to the country, living wherever he could on the hospitality and patronage of the landed gentry: first the Gooderes, later the family of Sir Walter Aston; at the end of his life he dedicated his last book (as "one of your family") to the Earl of Dorset. Between patrons, he could always count on the generosity of Goodere's daughter and her husband, the Rainsfords, at their country home near Stratford. He might also be engaged as a tutor for children of the gentry, such as the precocious Elizabeth Tanfield, one of the dedicatees of *England's Heroical Epistles*, the future Elizabeth Cary Viscountess Falkland. Such a life may sound unbearably parasitic to us, but Drayton and his hosts were simply continuing the traditional relationship of master and minstrel, at least insofar as it was maintained in those times, when most literary patronage had dwindled to a mean and temporary arrangement.

It is interesting to follow this old-fashioned young Drayton in the early 1590s as he makes his way in the literary world of the city. He experiments in all the fashionable kinds of verse—pastoral, sonnet, Ovidian complaint, and epyllion, at times with commendable success. After five years or so, having learned enough from these imitative sorties, he begins to go his own way.

Not much can be said for *The Harmony of the Church*:[5] a cento from Scripture was the sort of thing we might expect a country gentleman to encourage and a young country poet to undertake —safe, pious, and dull. In the address to the reader and the dedication to the "godly and virtuous" Lady Jane Devereux of Merivale, Drayton elects a defensive tone in the face of a sophisticated and not quite so godly and virtuous London audience. Lady Jane is asked to see his work "not as poems of poets, but prayers of prophets," and to be his "gracious patroness against any graceless parasite." The

"Address" that follows is equally self-righteous and in retrospect ironic: "I speak not of Mars, the god of Wars, nor of Venus, the goddess of love, but of the Lord of Hosts, that made heaven and earth. Not of toys in Mount Ida, but of triumphs in Mount Sion. Not of vanity, but of verity; not of tales, but of truths."

There is no reason to suppose that Drayton was anything but sincere in these protests, even though he would experiment with the toys of Mount Ida only two years later. The "Prayer of the Author" is taken from Ecclesiasticus, but the very fact of its selection enhances our picture of the naïve young poet, fresh from the country and most diffident about life in the great city:

> My Lord and God, from whom my life I took,
> Unto the wicked leave me not a prey;
> A haughty mind, a proud disdainful look,
> From me thy servant take thou clean away.

Drayton retained something of this rustic innocence even in later years when his style had become sophisticated; those who knew him always singled him out for his virtue, and he seems to have been one of the few practicing poets who stayed away from rioting and loose women.[6]

After two years he made his debut in secular poetry with his pastoral eclogues, *Idea The Shepherd's Garland*. In them he is obviously following Spenser, attempting his archaic diction, even dedicating the work to Robert Dudley, the son of Spenser's patron Leicester. Unfortunately, most of these poems have an unsettling stiffness and triteness about them, if only because Drayton's chief interest was in following the conventions and in paying tribute (to the Queen, Sidney, the Countess of Pembroke, and "Idea"). Later in life one of his favorite subjects for satire was the city, and the pastoral offered him a natural means of attacking urban vice; these early eclogues, however, make no such attempt, and are in fact quite inoffensive compared with Spenser's. Drayton is well informed about pastoral conventions, but has yet to make up his mind about pastoralism. All great pastoral poetry requires serious reflection over the nature of the pastoral life—the life of simplicity and peace as opposed to involvement and suffering. Both Spenser and Milton are skeptical of the life of withdrawal, while Theocritus seems to long for it; at this point in his life Drayton is not for it or against it, he simply hasn't thought about it.

Nevertheless, Drayton had much natural talent, and even in this stillborn child he managed to breathe a flicker of life. He enjoyed writing the seventh eclogue, which burlesques the diction of love-complaints: in Borrill's song he has ravaged his Textor to find over thirty epithets for "wretched love." The story of Dowsabel in the next eclogue will always be read, because it combines just the right proportions of appearance and reality in describing a love affair. Outwardly, Dowsabel is the usual simple maid who goes picking flowers in the traditional "pastourelle"; however, we are also told that she has studied "curtesie," wears green frocks, makes marzipan, and helps the priest say his matins on holy days. Nor is the young man in the woods a simple shepherd:

> This shepherd wore a sheep gray cloak,
> Which was of the finest loke,
> that could be cut with sheer,
> His mittens were of Bauzens skin,
> His cockers were of Cordiwin,
> his hood of Meniveere.[7]

In other words, he is too well dressed and she is too well versed to be what a reader might at first take them for. Her refusal and his protest are equally witty, particularly since she has tucked up her frock some thirty lines earlier:

> Sayth she yet lever were I dead,
> Than I should lose my maidenhead,
> and all for love of men:
> Sayth he yet are you too unkind,
> If in your heart you cannot find
> to love us now and then.

Drayton was principally a narrative artist, and in this kind, the short recreative verse-tale, he excelled, as witness *Nymphidia* and the comic fables of *The Moon-Calf*.

The second notable achievement in these early pastorals is the panegyric to Elizabeth, "Beta," in the third eclogue. It deliberately abounds in echoes of Spenser's "April" (Beta is the complement to Spenser's "Eliza"), and the flowers, Muses, and Ladies of the Lake are the stock in trade of Elizabeth's panegyrists. But a comparison between the two poems shows Drayton's Spenserianism to be only partial, reminding us that the younger poet wrote historical verse rather than Spenserian allegory—a difference that we can sense in the two poets' eclogues to the Queen. Throughout "April" Spenser displays his mythic inclination; Elizabeth is both the Queen and the archetypal monarch, and the allusion to "Latona's seed" serves as a meditation on the terrible powers that God has invested in the throne. Similarly, Henry VIII's romance with Ann Boleyn is idealized in the Pan-Syrinx fable, introducing not only the mystery of royalty's terrible power, but that of the beauty and goodness that result from a destructive act. In contrast with the wonder and mystery of "April," Drayton's song is rooted in admiration for the actual majesty of the Queen and her country. The birds and flowers are all English, and Beta is specifically Queen of the Thames; equally specific is the brazen patriotism of the closing stanza:

> Beta long may thine altars smoke, with yearly sacrifice,
> And long thy sacred temples may their Sabbaths solemnize,
> Thy shepherds watch by day and night,
> Thy maids attend the holy light,
> And thy large empire stretch her arms from east unto the west,
> And thou under thy feet mayst tread that foul seven-headed beast.

"April," then, is the work of an inspired *vates*, whereas the song to Beta is that of an aspiring poet laureate.

The stanza of this song is, so far as I have been able to discover, original with Drayton, and if so it is eminently suited to the stateliness required by its subject. One very similar to it is that of the eighth song in *Canzonets or Little Short Songs to Three Voices* by Thomas Morley, Gentleman of the Royal Chapel—a collection published the same year as *The Shepherd's Garland*. The coincidence is all the more noteworthy in that Morley's song is also used to pay tribute to the Queen:

> Blow, shepherds, blow your pipes with gladsome glee resounding.
> See where the fair Eliza comes with love and grace abounding.
> Run, Nymphs, apace, go meet her:
> With flowers and garlands greet her.
> All hail, Eliza fair, the country's pride and goddess:
> Long may'st thou live, the shepherd's Queen and lovely mistress.

Drayton's song would have fit Morley's music well, notwithstanding a slight variation in syllable-count. There is even a strong likelihood that Morley's song was written by Drayton, for Morley seldom put his own words to music. Drayton is usually identified as the "M. D." who wrote the commendatory verses to Morley's *First Book of Balletts to Five Voices* (1595), implying a friendship of some duration by that time. Aside from their prosodic similarities, the two songs are pastoral tributes to the Queen. The opening lines and the short lines of Drayton's stanzas vary in length just enough to suggest that he wrote his own song with a musical rather than metrical scheme in mind. Whatever the relation between songs, this poem of *The Shepherd's Garland* is by far the most musical of his early years, which may explain its inclusion in the popular anthology of pastoral lyrics, *England's Helicon*.[8]

The fifth eclogue, on the state of poetry, is central to *The Shepherd's Garland* not only in its position, but also in what it reveals about Drayton, or as he calls himself, Rowland. While it reflects the Spenserian ideals of "October" and *Mother Hubberd's Tale*, it anticipates Drayton's own mature thinking about poetry, as in the noble antiquarianism of Motto's opening stanza—the call for "the old stock of famous poesie," the rebuke of those who counterfeit the past ("forgers of supposed gentility"), the affirmation of honor impervious to fortune: "True valor lodgeth in the lowliest hearts, / Virtue is in the mind, not in th' attire." Rowland condemns the two kinds of poets whom Drayton always hated, the flatterer ("world's fawning fraud") with his emotional "brags of hope" and "sighs of base despair," and the slanderer, "Self-eating imp from viper's poison womb." Motto ends the dialogue by urging Rowland on to greater things—to "sing in honor of some worthy's deed"—thereby suggesting that (as was conventional) Drayton was already looking beyond pastoral to heroic poetry. The seriousness of purpose evinced in *The Harmony of the Church* has not dampened, of course; but in *The Shepherd's Garland* we may say that Drayton's youthful religious fervor has yielded somewhat in precedence to the secular values of honor, nobility, and national aspiration.

For reasons that may already be apparent, heroic poetry to Drayton meant historical poetry, and he finds his way into this kind in his "legends," poems in the *Mirror for Magistrates* tradition, which include *Peirs Gaveston* (1593 or 1594), *Matilda* (1594), *Robert of Normandy* (1596), and *The Legend of Great Cromwell* (1607). The first of these is not a good poem, but its dedication (to Henry Cavendish, another Warwickshire country gentleman) and postscript show us the historian latent in the poet. Drayton censures the "writers of these latter times" for their disagreement about Gaveston's character, "some omitting things worthy of memory, some inferring things without probability, disagreeing in many particulars, and cavelling in the circumstances of his sundry banishments." He adds that he has done his own research, "having recourse to some especial collections gathered by the industrious labors of John Stow, a diligent chronigrapher of our time."

Patient study does not guarantee literary success, however; *Gaveston* is a seriously flawed work not because of the author's scholarship but because of his choice of poetic convention. The Ovidian complaint, as it has been called, is a hybrid, deriving from the old tragic monologues of *The Mirror for Magistrates* and from the love complaints of Ovid's *Heroides*.[9] Even the first and best in this vogue, Daniel's *Complaint of Rosamond* (1592), does not escape the inherent, insuperable problem of reconciling Ovidian sensuousness with the somber gravity of the *Mirror* complaint. Moreover, in this poem Drayton found himself for the first time confronted with the task of a long narrative poem in which he had to manage character, incident, and setting, in addition to the themes of love and history.

At the very outset of *Gaveston*, we are reminded of the dual nature of its literary convention: the title character appears, "From gloomy shadow of eternal night," like all the damned ghosts of all the verse-tragedies before him. Yet in the fourth stanza an invocation suddenly dissipates the ghostly gloom: "O purple-buskined Pallas most divine, / Let thy bright fauchion lend me cypress boughs." We really find two Gavestons in the poem, one pagan-Ovidian, the other tragic-Stoic-Christian, and the failure to reconcile the two shows that Drayton was less than sensitive in his apprentice efforts at portraying a historical character. Although Gaveston first appears as a cringing fugitive "from Stygian lakes," in the closing stanzas his soul "is allowed her room among the blest," where, we are told, it had been waiting until summoned by the poet. Again, while at one point Gaveston longingly recalls his illicit love-affair with Edward, at another he appears shocked and wronged by accounts of their homosexuality.[10] Drayton acknowledges in his postscript that "Divers have been the opinions of the birth and first rising of Gaveston," and the contradictions in his own view of the king's favorite indicate that he himself could not accept one opinion for any length of time.

A revised *Gaveston* (1596) does not remove the faults of the first version, but it shows Drayton's efforts to improve the poem by giving it a more obvious moral direction. Each of the twenty-six new stanzas holds an ethical message or an outright condemnation of Gaveston's sins. Here as in the other legends published with this one, we may find a strengthening of the anti-Ovidian spirit, which culminates in the last, drastic revisions of 1605 and 1619, where the plain, direct style often echoes Baldwin's 1559 *Mirror*.

Both pastorals and legends were heavily influenced by the literary vogues of the nineties. Spenser, Daniel, and Lodge were the contemporary poets whom Drayton most admired and imitated at this time,[11] but the hands of Marlowe and Chapman are also visible in his work, particularly in *Endimion and Phoebe* (1595). Ostensibly, this is what modern scholars have called an epyllion, a mythological erotic tale told in the manner of Ovid; however, it departs from the pattern of *Hero and Leander* or *Venus and Adonis* in several particulars. It is the last poem of Drayton's apprentice years, for in it we see the veneer of imitativeness beginning to wear away.

Marlowe's *Hero and Leander* appeared in 1593 and Chapman's continuation not until five years later, though anyone who knew and respected Chapman as Drayton did could have seen those later "sestiads" in manuscript.[12] Drayton aligns himself with Marlowe and Chapman in writing his poem in heroic couplets rather than the stanzas of Lodge, Shakespeare, or Heywood; but more important, he deliberately manipulates the two poets' styles to emphasize the Platonic theme of *Endimion and Phoebe*—that the way to spiritual perfection begins in the study of the created universe. The opening tones are lush and Marlovian, depicting the physical beauty of the Arcadian paradise and the two lovers. The latter half of the poem gives way to "celestial things" and accordingly is dominated by a philosophical style evocative of Chapman. In effect, Drayton produces a new kind of poem, a philosophical epyllion: sexual love, the principal concern of earlier epyllions, is here a means to the end of communion with the beauty and truth of all nature.

Such a theme might have been apparent to any of Drayton's readers who were familiar with the old euhemeristic interpretation of the Endymion myth. Fulgentius had passed on the tradition that the moon-lover had actually been an astronomer, the first to discover the course of the moon. Because he devoted himself wholly to this investigation, he is said to have slept for thirty years.[18] Boccaccio later extended this interpretation: people say that Endymion slept because, in their foolish opinion, anyone who meditates on a subject, however lofty, might as well be asleep. Natalis Comes transmits this interpretation to the sixteenth century, explaining that Endymion was a man wholly given to deep speculation, not merely astronomy. This reading of the fable in Comes' much-used handbook would assure its wide circulation by Drayton's time.[14]

Endymion's ascent on the ladder of knowledge begins in the second half of the poem, almost at its mathematical center. Phoebe transports her lover:

> . . . up into her sphere,
> Imparting heavenly secrets to him there,
> Where lightened by her shining beams he sees
> The powerful planets, all in their degrees,
> Their sundry revolutions in the skies,
> And by their workings how they sympathize. (ll. 681–86)

Drayton argues that astronomical knowledge is the foundation of all natural learning, even the study of man, seeing that the stars exert so much influence upon

> . . . this little fleshly world of ours:
> Wherein her Maker's workmanship is found,
> As in contriving of this mighty round,
> In such strange manner and such fashion wrought,
> As doth exceed man's dull and feeble thought,
> Guiding us still by their directions. (ll. 698–703)

The closing triumphal progress introduces a long (perhaps too philosophical) digression on the correspondences, especially those in numbers of nine and three, "Into which numbers all things fitly fall."

Beside figuring the godhead and angelic choirs, three and nine constitute the numbers of the Graces and Muses, "To teach such as at poesy repine, / That it is only heavenly and divine."

At times in this poem Drayton shows a deep sensitivity to language and imagery; the opening lines, for example, have won many admirers. Still, it has the weaknesses of the other early poems: one feels that Drayton wished to follow in other poets' tracks, and to this motive he subordinated feelings and ideas that were truly his own. His talents were not for philosophical poetry, and decidedly not for the kind of heavy speculation in which Chapman engaged. Drayton is most like Chapman, and least like himself, in passages like this simile from *Endimion and Phoebe* (ll. 535–46):

> And as on him her fixed eyes were bent,
> So to and fro his color came and went;
> Like to a crystal near the fire set,
> Against the brightness rightly opposite,
> Now doth retain the color of the flame,
> And lightly moved again, reflects the same;
> For our affection quickened by her heat,
> Allayed and strengthened by a strong conceit,
> The mind disturbed forthwith doth convert,
> To an internal passion of the heart,
> By motion of that sudden joy or fear,
> Which . . .

and so on, for another nine lines. If there is any difference between the style of this and of Chapman's mad-schoolmasterly *Shadow of Night* (1594), it is in the relative smoothness of Drayton's verses. Drayton shared Chapman's faith in the ennobling effects of learning, his contempt for the vulgar and the merely erotic. However, he was ill-equipped and ultimately not inclined to deal in Platonic obscurities. *Endimion and Phoebe*, though it has its charming flights, was on the whole an experiment that failed, and it is a mark of Drayton's self-critical abilities that he chose not to publish the poem again.[15]

Sonnets

Idea's Mirror, Drayton's first sonnets, appeared in 1594, and ought properly to have been considered earlier, if the ordering of this survey were strictly chronological. However, for what they reveal about their author, the sonnets of 1594 are properly to be read in the light of the massive surgery that they underwent in 1599 and later years. These revisions measure more faithfully than any other poetry how much Drayton had learned in the school of the Elizabethans.

Because the 1594 sonnets are so obviously in the fashion of Sidney's and Daniel's sonnets (printed just three years earlier), we must understand as a mere formality Drayton's claim that they had long "slept in sable night." True, some verses do recall the graceless amateur of *The Harmony of the Church*—such as the lolloping alexandrines with feminine rhyme in Amour 17, which Drayton later omitted; but if there was much delay at all before sending the sonnets to press it was probably owing to the lack of a patron to finance their printing. (This "ever-kind Maecenas" was yet another Warwickshire gentleman, Anthony Cook.)

We should expect to hear echoes of *Astrophil and Stella* in these first sonnets, for Drayton venerated Sidney's memory all his life. Many of the sonnets develop the Sidneian theme of the conflict between reason and passion, such as Amour 31, the most Sidneian of the lot, a perfect counterfeit of the master's style:

> Sitting alone, Love bids me go and write;
> Reason plucks back, commanding me to stay,
> Boasting that she doth still direct the way,
> Else senseless Love could never once indite.

Drayton's editors see a source in *Astrophil and Stella* 10; but the influence is more general than that. Drayton has learned the use of personification in sonnets from Sidney, as well as the symmetrical "building" of each poem. One quatrain being given to Reason, a second must go to Love:

> Love, growing angry, vexed at the spleen,
> And scorning Reason's maimed argument,
> Straight taxeth Reason, wanting to invent
> Where she with Love conversing hath not been.

Expanding this personification into an *allegoria*, as Sidney so often does, the third quatrain shows the two opponents converging:

> Reason, reproached with this coy disdain,
> Despiteth Love, and laugheth at her folly,
> And Love, contemning Reason's reason wholly,
> Thought her in weight too light by many a grain.

The final couplet, the pinnacle of this symmetrical construction, yokes the opposing terms in an ingenious pun:

> Reason, put back, doth out of sight remove,
> And Love alone finds reason in my love.

In the personification and the struggle with the divided self, Amour 31 contains the germ of the 1619 sonnet "Since there's no help," but it is still a long way from the perfection of Drayton's finest lyric.

Other poems of *Idea's Mirror* are even less distinguished in their conventionality. The sequence opens with a disavowal of "these rude unpolished rhymes," which the poet has at last decided to show the world, and with fervent hopes that his patron will be able to enhance them by the grace of his name. This prefatory sonnet concludes with an assertion of independence from literary influence—in itself an out-and-out falsehood, which can only be justified in that it, too, was conventional. The main body of the sonnets unfortunately lives up to our expectations, from the book-conceit of the first sonnet ("Read here (sweet maid) the story of my woe") to the envoy of Amour 51 ("Go you, my lines, ambassadors of love"). The tenth amour begins:

> Oft taking pen in hand, with words to cast my woes,
> Beginning to account the sum of all my cares,

a mere retreading of Daniel's

> . . . book of my charged soul,
> Where I have cast th' account of all my care:
> Here have I summed my sighs, . . .

which had at least departed from the tenor of *Astrophil and Stella* 18:

> With what sharp checks I in myself am shent
> When into Reason's audit I do go,
> And by just counts myself a bankrout know
> Of all those goods which heaven to me hath lent.

Drayton provides the usual catalogues of antitheses ("Those tears which quench my hope still kindle my desire") and the same apostrophes as the other sonneteers, including one to "Black pitchy night," which looks back to Sidney's sonnet "O night the ease of care" in the *Arcadia*, and to Daniel's "Care-charmer sleep" in *Delia*.

As an index to Drayton's interests, however, the 1594 sequence is of some value, for scattered through the conventional chaff are a few grains of the artist's own personality. In the two sonnets to the Ankor River (13 and 24) the customary praise of the mistress is merely a pretext for praise of the English countryside: the second of these is a roll call of the principal rivers in England, anticipating *Poly-Olbion* in the manner of personification (the regions "vaunt" and "commend" their rivers), and even in the order in which the rivers are presented. Of course it was not unusual to associate the sonnet mistress with a particular locality: Sidney has an address to the Thames on seeing Stella pass there, and one of Daniel's sonnets rejects the Thames (London) for the Avon ("where Delia hath her seat"). But rarely among English or continental sonnet writers does one find a sonnet so thoroughly "chorographical" as Amour 24. Amour 13 ("Clear Ankor, on whose silver-sanded shore") is implicitly a love-song to the rural woodland of Drayton's home. The final couplet, "Fair Arden, thou my Tempe art alone, / And thou, sweet Ankor, art my Helicon" expresses a notion that is, as we have already seen, fundamental in Drayton: that the literature, the learning, the nobility, even the natural beauty of England could surpass that of any other country, ancient or modern. This is also the thought behind Amour 19, in which a Sibylline Idea excels "her of Delphos or Cumaea," and Amour 20, where Idea is a wonder surpassing the "hills and floods" of ancient fame.

When we compare these early sonnets with the revisions of 1599, we are impressed by Drayton's growth in judgment. The improvement is partly attributable to his writing for the theater. Since at least 1597 he had been collaborating on plays for the Admiral's men, or Worcester's company, and the experience gave his style a markedly greater range and flexibility than it had possessed in the earlier nineties. In place of the artificial, patterned language of Amour 39,

> Die, die, my soul, and never taste of joy,
> If sighs, nor tears, nor vows, nor prayers can move;

> If faith and zeal be but esteemed a toy,
> And kindness be unkindness in my love,

we find the subdued rhythms of natural speech:

> Love in an humor played the prodigal,
> And bids my senses to a solemn feast,
> Yet more to grace the company withal,
> Invites my heart to be the chiefest guest. (*Idea*, Sonnet 7)

In the sonnet to the reader, Drayton himself affirms this break with Petrarchan clichés:

> No far-fetch'd sigh shall ever wound my breast,
> Love from mine eye a tear shall never wring,
> Nor in ah-me's my whining sonnet's dressed.

With the rejection of the old style comes attention to new subjects. Fully a third of the sonnets newly introduced in 1599 have nothing to do with passion or reason or love: there are some on poetry (2, 3, 31, 46), on astronomy (11, 23), on religion (13, 14), even on the national language (25).

Another important influence, though it does not come until a decade or so later, was the style of Donne and his circle.[16] A comparison of the earlier and later sonnets may of itself be sufficient to convince some that Drayton learned from the witty and colloquial manner of Donne, and the argument is enhanced when we go beyond the sonnets to find abundant evidence of Metaphysical influence. Here, for example, is a passage from the original seduction speech of King John as it appeared in the 1594 *Matilda*:

> Shine thou like Cynthia under mine estate,
> Thy tresses deckt with Ariadne's crown,
> In pomp redoubling costly Juno's rate,
> And cloud the world in sable with a frown. (ll. 400–3)

These lines, and dozens like them, are struck out in the *Matilda* of 1605 and 1619. Where the King had earlier spoken of "orient pearl" and "rarest unicorn," he now tempts Matilda with sophistry:

> Hoard not thy beauty, when thou hast such store:
> Wer't not great pity it should thus lie dead,
> Which by the lending might be made much more? (ll. 232–34)

The inspiring force of the first passage is the rhetoric of Marlowe, the early Shakespeare, the "Petrarchans"; that of the second, the love poems of Donne and his circle, with their wry logic and the accenting of sense over sound. The later elegies also reveal such influence: one of them, "Of His Lady's Not Coming to London," is in fact a unique attempt to write Ovidian elegy in the Donne manner. The poem "Upon the Death of His Incomparable Friend Sir Henry Rainsford," written between 1622 and 1627, opens with lines characteristically metaphysical in their immediacy and their conversational tone:

> Could there be words found to express my loss,
> There were some hope, that this my heavy cross
> Might be sustained, and that wretched I
> Might once find comfort.

It might be argued that this is simply the plain style required of funeral elegy, but in the "plain" poets of an earlier generation, like Lord Vaux or Ralegh, one finds plain sententiousness rather than the intimate simplicity of these lines. As with most of Drayton's elegies, the voice, the structure, the movement of the lines in this poem bear the impress of Donne's epistles, elegies, and satires.

Now, if the metaphysical vogue did influence Drayton, why did he persist in such an unmetaphysical enterprise as the sonnet sequence? The sonnet vogue was virtually defunct by 1599, so that by 1619, when the finest sonnets appear, the fashionable set in London must have thought them terribly dated. Only two other important Jacobean poets, neither of whom was English, continued in the wake of *Astrophil and Stella*: Sir William Alexander and William Drummond. The urbane Ben Jonson told the latter that his poems "were not after the fancy of the time." If Drayton had merely continued reissuing his sonnets from the nineties, we could attribute his tenacity to any number of simple motives; but the *Idea* sonnets are a notorious instance of his penchant for revising, adding to, and subtracting from his published work. Sonnets retained from 1594 in the final 1619 text are sometimes the result of five distinct phases of emendation. More important than the question of fashionableness is the fact that after 1600 Drayton concentrates on historical poetry and other long narrative kinds, which ought to have lured him away from writing sonnets.

The reason for his persistence may on the surface seem gratuitous: he simply revered the sonnet tradition, as he did all English traditions. For this aging Elizabethan the sonnet represented a bridge across the decades into the age of Sidney,

> That heroë for numbers and for prose
> That throughly pac'd our language as to show
> That plenteous English hand in hand might go
> With Greek and Latin . . . .[17]

At least in this one instance in Drayton's poetry, the medium *is* the message. Although he was quick to apply the lessons of the drama or of Donne's circle to his own style, that style existed within a deeply rooted allegiance to the English poetic tradition. Like pastoral and verse-tragedy, the sonnet had held a venerable place in the tradition when he first came to know it, and he was not about to abandon it for the novelties of the forum. In all likelihood his respect for Drummond and Alexander was in great measure due to their fidelity to the same tradition.

The final sonnets of 1619 reflect no particular mood, but deliberately oscillate between pious idealism and wry cynicism, between melancholy and merriment. I maintain this view despite the intriguing argument by Walter R. Davis that "*Idea* is essentially a comic sonnet-sequence, its subject the unsuccessful attempt to avoid conventionality."[18] True, we cannot take seriously the tongue-in-cheek rantings of "Thou purblind boy" and "Cupid, I hate thee," which invoke a tradition at least as ancient as Catullus (*Carmen* XI); similarly the abuse of the lady in "There's nothing grieves me" and "What dost thou mean" mocks the speaker in its peevish excess. But both the prefatory sonnet "To the Reader" and the new opening sonnet of 1619 call our attention to another mood in the speaker, namely his penchant for variety:

> My verse is the true image of my mind,
> Ever in motion, still desiring change;
> And as thus to variety inclined,
> So in all humors sportively I range.
> My Muse is rightly of the English strain,
> That cannot long one fashion entertain.

Like other collections of lyric verse in this period, the later sonnets are defined neither by one sustained emotion nor by any single love affair. A handful of them indeed stand entirely out of the amorous context (e.g., Sonnets 11, 12, 25, and 32), while a poem like "Dear, why should you commend me" exudes a cool intimacy in which the comic can have no place. If there is any consistent voice in these newest sonnets, it is that announced in Sonnet 1—of the old "sea-farer" who has experienced all, and takes whatever comes along, dropping a few curses along the way. The much-acclaimed "Since there's no help," another addition to the 1619 sequence, is best read with this kind of voice in mind. The lover in the opening two lines is not really possessed by a divided mind; with his melodramatic *allegoria* he is simply putting up a front. Love and passion are near death, but they can come back anytime they are wanted. Perhaps it is our remoteness from seventeenth-century medical practices that lets us believe it possible to recover so quickly from an illness that is not being faked.

Except in their traditionalism the sonnets are not representative of Drayton, but viewed across their three-decade history they exemplify in a limited space the history of Drayton's artistic development. He begins in the nineties as an imitator, then toward the end of that decade he finds his own voice. From that point on there is a continuing improvement, a craftsman's attention to the sound and sense of language, a greater diversity of style, subject, and mood. When the finished product finally arrives, it is splendid: for once, at least, the poet was made, not born.

Drayton's Patriotism

If the *Oxford English Dictionary* is correct, the words *patriot* and *national* first entered our language in 1596 and 1597. In other words, the very concept that inspired Drayton's principal works grew to maturity with him. The origins of Renaissance patriotism have been listed often: anti-clericalism, mercantile competition, the prosperity of free cities, the rediscovery of antiquity, the invention of gunpowder, printing, and the compass—all contributed to the massive change in self-awareness that Western nations underwent during the fifteenth and sixteenth centuries. In England the emergent national character was particularly affected by a devastating series of civil wars in the fifteenth century, which severely weakened the old nobility and allowed Tudor rulers to establish in its stead a more pliant aristocracy, including a large new class of ambitious gentlemen who were employed to administer the new dynasty's autocratic designs. Gradually, though the whole process by which the power shifted was barely discernible in its stages, this new class came to have more to say in the shaping of these designs than the peerage and the monarchs themselves.

The government's designs naturally included territorial expansion and the development of new maritime commercial schemes, and in both efforts it found success. Comparing England in 1400 and in 1600, one sees a remote and impotent nation transformed into a first-rank sea power, reckoned by her greatest enemies as the champion of protestant Europe. Already, during the fifteenth-century French wars, England was discovering what Shaw called "her peculiar fitness to rule over less civilized races for their own good." By the mid-sixteenth century, having at last given up on the French, the nation turned her imperial aspirations to Ireland, a land that first nourished the colonialism of proto-imperialists like Drake and Ralegh. After some remarkable naval successes, not the least of which was owing to simple luck, the notion took hold that Britannia was destined to rule the waves. In other words, the seeds of English patriotism and the British empire were planted together, so that it is not always possible to tell where one leaves off and the other begins.

If the last two decades of Elizabeth's reign witnessed an increase in colonial and maritime activity, they also gave rise to a more fervid brand of patriotism, largely a result of the nation's instinct for survival. The struggle against an enemy had prompted some of the most spirited expressions of patriotism in the Renaissance, from Petrarch's "Italia mia" to Ronsard's "Remontrance au Peuple de France." On the sea, at least, the great English enemy from the 1560s on was Spain, and every young Englishman who could not go to sea, but who turned out for the increasingly frequent musters of the Queen's militia, could at least in his dreams partake in the romance of defending the fatherland. The foreign threat acted sharply upon men's political consciousness, frequently converting passive citizens into aggressive patriots—how sharply may be seen in the example of Drayton's boyhood master, Henry Goodere. In 1568 a romantic young Goodere carried some messages for the fugitive Queen of Scots, for which he was briefly imprisoned in the Tower. By 1592, however, Goodere was an ardent anti-papist, hunting down Catholic recusants in Warwickshire. He adopted the later role after a term of military service in the Netherlands, and after the great threat of the Armada, when Goodere was appointed a colonel in the Queen's defense forces. If in his mature life Drayton did not quite share the vehemence of the older man's anti-Romanism, it was only because, with the strengthening of the Anglican church and the diminution of the Spanish threat, such zeal seemed no longer expedient. Drayton's generation inherited the patriotism of Sir Henry's, but found new channels for expressing it, one of which lay in the sea lanes. From the seventies to the nineties a subtle but palpable shift occurs in the arena of heroism: from the circle of military achievement to that of voyages, discoveries, and daring feats at sea. When James I took measures to discourage such adventures, he naturally incurred the odium of a vast number of his subjects, Drayton prominently among them.

The main external influence on Drayton's patriotism was not fear of Spain or hostility to the crown, but the attitudes of his social class. Country gentlemen naturally made up the bulk of the English governing class in this heavily agricultural nation, and lent impetus to the patriotic solidarity that prevailed during most of Elizabeth's reign. Drayton's life-long ties with the "Country," especially the rural gentry of the Midlands, paralleled his love of the English countryside. He retained these ties despite a crucial series of changes in the gentry's political attitudes, which were to culminate in the Country-supported rebellion of the 1640s. In Drayton's youth neither he nor his contemporaries would have anticipated this split between Country and Court or City, so united did England appear under her popular Queen. Toward the end of the century, intercourse between the shires and London was eased with the introduction of private coaches for conveying gentlemen and their ladies to London,[19] where fine clothes, plays, and Court-news became increasingly abundant. But the new attention to city life took its toll in the country: the absentee landlord often neglected his tenants or forced them to pay higher rents to support his city extravagances. Bad harvests and economic uncertainties played a part in the decline, but there is no denying Drayton's charge in his satires that sheer folly led men to forget much that was good and holy, however dull, in England at large.

By the time of James I a rift had developed in the society, which the King was powerless to understand, let alone heal. Aligned against the rural population, in the eyes of many, were the courtiers with the lawyers and merchants of London.[20] It was a tragic ending to the history of Elizabethan patriotism. The politics of the Country soon began to take on a reactionary character, branding as heinous the newfangleness of City and Court wits, deploring their fashions in hair and clothes, longing for the good old days of Queen Elizabeth, who knew the value of a penny and the worth of a plain Englishman. By the time of James's death, patriotism, which in the 1580s and 1590s had permeated all walks of English society, had become the rallying position of a large, if somewhat ill-defined, rural citizenry.

The tendency of patriotism to become, in the early seventeenth century, the special prerogative of the Country is best indicated by the fact that the only poets who have any claim to be called "patriotic" are men with strong Country affiliations—Drayton, George Wither, and William Browne. Ben Jonson, a special case in the public poetry of the age (see Appendix B), grows increasingly resentful of his fellow Londoners, and in his mature years the City gives way in his drama to the woodland world of *The Sad Shepherd* —a move anticipated in such earlier poems as "To Penshurst" and "To Mary Lady Wroth" (Epigram 105), which reflect a deep sympathy with the ways of the country manor. Conversely, most poets with a London or Court background tend to avoid any poetic expression of national pride. Under Elizabeth a London poet had been able to wave a flag as well as any man: Spenser is the supreme example, but witness also George Peele's "Farewell to Sir John Norris and Sir Francis Drake" (1589) and Chapman's "De Guiana" (1596). To Donne and his followers America was useful as matter for a conceit, but little else. Robert Herrick is often hailed for his "country" charm, but Herrick's mood is that of a London wit among the rustics taking in the local color and the local milkmaids. Except in flattery Herrick seldom ventures into the world of affairs, and even his encomia reveal a certain naïvety about the politics of his society.[21] When Drayton, in his preface to *Poly-Olbion*, reproaches the "idle humorous world," he obviously has in mind the audience of these urban sophisticates, who "had rather read the fantasies of foreign inventions, than to see the rarities and history of their own country delivered by a true native Muse."

It is especially appropriate that Drayton should deplore the neglect of history, for history is inevitably the domain of the patriotic poet. In any society such poets are called to two kinds of subjects: the deeds of great men, and the failure of the present to continue on the path of greatness. In primitive societies these impulses take the form of memorial poetry, frequently consisting simply in the names of the venerable dead, and taunts or gibes, which may be carried out quite as ceremoniously as the memorial kind. Greek myth enshrines Mnemosyne or Memory as the mother of the Muses because poetry and art arouse memories of past greatness, and thereby conserve this knowledge—thus, in Pindar Mnemosyne is the giver of fame.[22] Because Drayton saw the office of the poet as a public one, the bulk of his writing carries out these two ancient functions, either as commemorative (mostly historical) poetry or satire. It is generally agreed that he is the chief historical poet of the English Renaissance,[23] but his satire is often overlooked. The two kinds are complementary, for as a historical poet Drayton is always concerned to project England's history into her present, while as a satirist he inevitably depends on traditional values as a standard of excellence—in morality, in government, and in poetry. Later in his career, the satirist's indignation frequently emerges even in the nonsatiric works, showing how fully he shared the outrage of other literate rural Englishmen under the Stuarts. He voiced their sense that ambitious, self-serving men had subverted the "English" traditions of their forefathers, and it is not difficult to imagine him in their ranks had he lived into the troubled 1640s, when the Puritans canonized Elizabeth and Ralegh, and when Cromwell renewed if only for a moment the old Queen's pattern of government.[24]

2 | LESSONS OF THE PAST

There is a history in all men's lives,
Figuring the nature of the times deceased;
The which observed, a man may prophesy,
With a near aim, of the main chance of things
As yet not come to life, which in their seeds
And weak beginnings lie intreasured.

(Warwick in *2 Henry IV*   III.i)

Historians in Verse

Only one other poet can rival Drayton's claim to pre-eminence in historical poetry during his time, Samuel Daniel, whose lengthy *Civil Wars* had an indisputable influence on Drayton, though as we shall see, its effect was not always salutary. Yet unlike any of Drayton's historical poems, *The Civil Wars* was never completed, and later in life Daniel simply gave up writing history in verse, preferring prose as the medium for his *History of England*. Drayton alludes to his rival in the genre only once, in the elegy to Reynolds:

Amongst these Samuel Daniel, whom if I
May speak of, but to censure do deny,
Only have heard some wisemen him rehearse,
To be too much Historian in verse;
His rhymes were smooth, his meters well did close,
But yet his manner better fitted prose. (ll. 123–28)

These remarks are usually read as a slur on Daniel, but they need not be. The last couplet is consistent with the whole passage if we see it not as a disparagement of Daniel's poetic skill (the first couplet precludes that meaning) but as a comment on the kind of history Daniel wrote. Although he was indeed a "smooth" and graceful poet—not prosaic, as we now think of the term—the kind of history he wrote was better suited to prose than poetry. Daniel, a more philosophical man than Drayton, especially preoccupied with the nature of poetry and history, had very probably come to the same conclusion years before the elegy to Reynolds—indeed, this is one explanation of his shift from verse to prose.[1]

In general, the relations between poetry and history had been in a state of flux for more than a hundred years. During the fifteenth century the alliance between the two arts, assumed since the beginning of the Middle Ages, had grown increasingly uneasy. There had been a time when "storie" meant indiscriminately either historical or fictional narrative, but that was in an age notoriously deficient in its sense of the past. Yet even in the Quattrocento one finds humanist commentaries tending still to view history and poetry as amicable, if different, branches of rhetoric: the historian, like the poet, must select and organize his material, and must write with an ethical purpose or theme in mind.[2] With the Cinquecento rediscovery of Aristotle's *Poetics* comes a renewal of the ancient argument that the poet is superior to the historian because he deals in universals. Historians, on the other hand, begin asserting their independence and excellence over the poets, and develop an esteem for good scholarship and sound principles of evidence that contrasts with the gullibility and advocacy of earlier chroniclers. The first Tudor historians develop a selective sense in their works which marks an improvement over the rambling medieval chronicles, though this new selectivity did not always allow for an honest, scholarly use of sources: advocacy still flourished in the writings of Polydore Vergil, Edward Hall, and John Foxe.[3]

Nevertheless, in the thinking of Drayton's time, the difference between history in prose and in verse seems to have been largely a matter of degree. All historians then would have agreed with the first professor of modern history at Oxford, Degory Wheare, that "History is nothing but moral philosophy clothed in examples."[4] Because moral truth was the shaping principle of history, facts, often well-known facts, could be distorted or overlooked for the sake of the nobler end. But at this point historical prose and verse seem to part company. Especially by the seventeenth century, prose historians were much more critical of their sources than their counterparts in verse, more careful in their inferences, and generally averse to inserting things that were not there, such as "feigned orations" and dramatic monologues.[5] Poet-historians, on the other hand (including writers of historical drama), tended toward what we today call historical romance, though as always they wrote with an ethical intent, not just to entertain. Poetry, in mixing the useful with the sweet, was universally expected to fabricate, to idealize, even to distort; a reader who wanted facts was better advised to look to the chroniclers or the newer breed of historians like Guicciardini and Machiavelli. As the first Elizabethan historical poet wrote, "It is lawful to poets to feign what they lyst, so it be appertinent to the matter."[6]

A useful illustration of this difference may be seen in Drayton's treatment of his sources in *The Barons' Wars*. In this poem about the reign of Edward II, the focus is on the dangers of factionalism, ambition, and civil war, and to emphasize his theme Drayton cancels out those facts of the reign that might blur the point. For example, prose historians recognized the dangerous Queen Isabel as a prime instigator of Edward's troubles; in John Stow's *Annals of England* (1592) she is a real ogress, as in her treatment of Hugh Spencer:

> After this the Queen with her people came to Gloucester, from whence she went unto Bristow, where Hugh Spencer the elder committed himself and all his unto the mercy of the angry and outrageous woman, who commanded the earl to be bound, and without question [i.e., judicial examination] to be drawn and hanged in his armor, taken down alive and bowelled, his bowels burned, then his head smitten off, and his body hanged up again, and after four days to be cut all to pieces and cast to dogs to be eaten, but his head was sent to Winchester.[7]

In *The Barons' Wars* Hugh Spencer's execution gets passing notice, the culprits go unnamed, and Isabel herself is not associated with the incident. By the same token, at a later point in Stow's *Annals*, the Queen herself orders her husband's execution, while in Drayton the fatal message comes from an unidentified "they."[8] Recalling that Drayton was Stow's friend and admirer, and that he himself took pride in his historical research, we may be somewhat puzzled by the disparity in so important a matter as the Queen's personal involvement in these atrocities. Clearly, Drayton does not tell the full truth about Isabel because it would only distract his reader from the moral truth governing his whole poem: that the responsibility for the horrors of Edward II's reign lay collectively with the Court and the factious nobility.

Virtually all Elizabethan historical writing assumes that the actions of men, good and evil, are part of a divinely established pattern; even Ralegh, for all his secularism, held that "God, who is the author of all our tragedies, hath written out for us and appointed for us all the parts we are to play."[9] The root cause of national greatness or disaster was invariably agreed to be Providence, even when it was called Fortune, Fate, or Destiny.[10] History in verse tended to emphasize as corollary to the providential idea the notion that history must repeat itself. The City of Man consisted of beings whose nature was fixed, predictable, and more than a little depraved: hence Warwick's lines, quoted as epigraph to this chapter. That seminal body of Elizabethan historical poetry, *The Mirror for Magistrates*, exposes on the individual human level the theory that all mankind is involved in a continuing cycle of ascent, descent, and resurrection. Shakespeare, Drayton, and Daniel lend a national dimension to this view by projecting the Plantagenet past on the Tudor present. The usefulness of their historical poetry lay partly in its admonitory function, and as government officials in fact recognized, the spate of poems and plays in late Elizabethan England dealing with the reigns of Edward II and Richard II was meant to comment as much on the present as on the past. When he died in 1595, Lord Burghley, not a man for idle research, left six pages of notes on Edward II's reign, listing the friends and enemies of the Crown.[11]

Although Ralegh observed that "we may gather out of history a policy no less wise than eternal,"[12] Elizabethan history, especially historical poetry, was not really an inferential activity. The poet himself brought the design to history, sharpening the outlines, and putting in color for the audience. Thus, the lessons of Providence were dictated by the character of Elizabethan poets and their society, and a little reading in the poems and plays of the period suggests that these lessons were few and simple.

Foremost was the need for national unity and the danger of ambition and self indulgence. Daniel's maxim, "Times of faction, times of slander be,"[13] is a pervading theme in his *Civil Wars*, and factionalism breeds most of the political ills in Shakespeare's history plays. The somber mood of the *Henry VI* plays derives from England's gradual loss of prestige and territory, which is directly attributed to factions; on the other hand, *Henry V* and the anonymous *Edward III* are joyful plays because the united efforts of all Englishmen result in victory. Second only to factionalism as a cause of national disaster was foreign political influence: one need hardly elaborate on the xenophobia that trod the London stage from John Bale to Shakespeare. In *Henry VI* the foreign devils are Joan and Margaret. The usurping Lords Scroop and Grey in *Sir John Oldcastle* obtain offers of men and money from France to overthrow Henry V. In the anonymous *Woodstock*—a propaganda piece on the values of the rural English gentry as contrasted with the corruptions and extravagance of the Court—a frivolous Richard II plots to eliminate his opposition and seek aid from abroad against his own people.

The historical poets also see Providence as working through great men, and in this respect betray the influence of the Old Testament historians upon the popular imagination. Courage, piety, wisdom—the virtues of Saul, David, and Solomon—are enshrined in great rulers like Henry V. That Elizabethans held a personalist view of history goes without saying, but it was the peculiar strength of historical poetry, in particular historical drama, that it could present, as discursive prose could not, the character of the great man: on the stage power and fame—those two great Elizabethan obsessions—moved vividly before the eye, lending a ritual moment of wonder to the poor, drab lives of the spectators. Majesty had never held such awe in medieval England, when its power was diffused through the various levels of the feudal order: Spenser's "April" and Shakespeare's history plays could only have been written in Tudor England. From the meditations of *The Mirror for Magistrates* to the battle scenes of *Henry V*, poets taught the same lesson: that the great goal of ordinary men was to fulfill the destiny of their nation through submission to holy, zealous, and powerful leaders.

Historical poetry, then, had an immense social function in Elizabethan times: it was not mere antiquarianism, like much of the prose (Stow's *Survey of London*, for example, or Camden's *Britannia*); it may best be described as monumental history,[14] the effort to derive a pattern of greatness from contemplation of the past. More important than its admonitory purpose (which may seem unduly emphasized in this discussion) was its epideictic function. The monumental historian, through the vision of the past, reminds his audience that greatness, having been possible once, may be so again. He is thus by definition a patriotic poet. Of course the weakness of this historical mode is the weakness of all Elizabethan historical poetry, Drayton's included: it always skirts the gray margin of fiction, tending to idealize effects without regard to causes. For the critical mind (which is not without its own dangers) monumental history is finally unconvincing, even insipid, and the decline of historical poetry and drama in the seventeenth century may be traced directly to the decline of faith and the advance of reason, foreshadowed in one of England's first "modern" historians, Sir Francis Bacon.

Mortimeriados and *The Barons' Wars*

Drayton's *Mortimeriados* (1596) follows Daniel's *Civil Wars* by only a year, one reason why the two poets' names are often linked. Yet a glance at the two works shows no basis for confusing them. *The Civil Wars* is a poem without a hero, like Shakespeare's *Henry VI*—or if there is a hero it is England herself. This is not to say that Daniel's work—which moves from the fall of Richard II to that of Edward IV—is any less modern as history than *Mortimeriados*, for in his attention to factual details and in his analysis of events Daniel was the more sophisticated. Drayton, by contrast, limiting his scope to a single event, the rise and fall of Roger Mortimer, provided dramatic unity to his work, which the "prose" historian Daniel could not achieve.

To say that Mortimer is the "hero" of the poem is somewhat misleading, for Drayton follows Marlowe's *Edward II* in making King Edward and Mortimer a study in contrasts. As in the play, we find ourselves resenting the King in the first half of the poem and sympathizing with him in the latter—in each case with the opposite response to Mortimer. When Drayton revised the poem as *The Barons' Wars* in 1602, he intensified the contrast between the two by making a sharp temporal division of seven years in the middle of the poem. In this new version Mortimer is taken prisoner in the last canto of both halves: in Canto III he is imprisoned in the Tower of London, and in Canto VI he is seized in another tower, in the Queen's bedchamber. The third and sixth cantos of the new version are nearly all given to love story, while the first and second, fourth and fifth, focus on political and military action. At the end of Canto III Mortimer is a heroic fugitive and the victorious King a villain; at the close of Canto VI we pity the repentant King and are repelled by the excesses to which the usurping Mortimer and Isabel have fallen. Although the same cycle governs both versions (disorder, chaos, the death of the old King, the restoring of order in the new Edward), the effect of the 1602 revisions is to make this symmetry more evident.

Perhaps it is the nature of Drayton's work as poetic rather than prose history that has led some to feel that the poet is less interested than Marlowe, Shakespeare, and Daniel in the national issues upon which his history turns.[15] A great deal can be said for the opposite point of view. The very subject of the poem, civil war, had been vexing Elizabethans who saw the religious strife of earlier decades now compounded by the problem of succession. In *Mortimeriados* Drayton's concern on this point elicits a long apostrophe to the English (of both past and present) on the verge of a civil war:

> O warlike Nation hold thy conquering hand,
> Even senseless things do warn thee yet to pause,
> Thy mother soil on whom thy feet do stand,
> O then infringe not Nature's sacred laws. (ll. 295-98)

Look at the "Eagles, lions, talbots, bears" on your shields, he tells the warring factions: "Those beasts you bear do in their kinds agree,/ And than those beasts more savage will you be?" Finally, he points out the domestic perversity of civil war:

> What, shall the sister weep her brother's death,
> Who sent her husband to his timeless grave?
> The nephew moan his uncle's loss of breath,
> Which did his father of his life deprive?
> Who shall have mind your memories to save?
> Or shall he burial to his friend afford,
> Who lately put his son unto the sword? (ll. 323–29)

At the threshold of England's greatest crime during the war, the murder of the King, Drayton's lines are full of contemporary significance—deliberately ambiguous in reference to "this rebellious, hateful, iron age."[16] Here, though the ostensible subject is the plight of Mortimer's London, we are also to read an allusion to the religious infighting of the 1590s:

> The place profan'd where God should be ador'd,
> The stone remov'd whereon our faith is grounded,
> Authority is scorn'd, counsel abhor'd,
> Religion so by foolish sects confounded
> Weak consciences by vain questions wounded:
> The honor due to Magistrates neglected,
> What else but vengeance can there be expected? (ll. 1513–19)

The passage ends with a stanza of admonition (although the sense is somewhat obscure):

> Time, end thyself here, let it not be said,
> That ever Death did first begin in thee,
> Nor let this slander to thy fault be laid,
> That ages charge thee with impiety,
> Lest fear what hath been argue what may be:
> And fashioning so a habit of the mind,
> Make men no men, and alter human kind. (ll. 1611–17)

These lines may be paraphrased roughly as follows: "Unhappy age, now your calamities have been recalled, but let men not say (because they secretly fear that your wickedness may forebode the same evils to come in later times) that you were the only age cursed by death and wickedness. Whoever so discounts the possibility of such evil happening again forms a habit of mind which is oblivious to the eternal, predictable element in human nature." In other words, if it happened then, gentle reader, it can happen now. The evils of Edward's day—political and religious factions, self-serving politicians and foreign intriguers—are all present in 1596, not to mention the generally deplored (and perhaps deplorable) state of public morals. These are the national issues, then, of which Drayton is fully cognizant, and to convert *Mortimeriados* into an unpolitical adventure story is simply to discount several hundred lines of authorial comment on the action.

In *Mortimeriados* Drayton for the first time takes up a subject that was to hold his attention for the next decade, the relation between national destiny and the personal human spirit. *The Barons' Wars, England's Heroical Epistles,* and *Cromwell* constitute an attempt to reconcile the obvious greatness of England with the equally obvious fact that many of her great men were scoundrels. Reconciliation is never really accomplished, nor could it have been: Sidney had deplored the fact that in history bad men do succeed and that the historian is unable to alter the past. Nevertheless, the poet-historian Drayton offered a fictional justification of the past by selecting for his villains men who, despite their malign influence, inadvertently brought good to England. Mortimer helped rid the Court of its profligacy, Cromwell assisted in the expulsion of popery. Both wrongdoers paid for their crimes, as did those in the *Epistles* (William de la Poole wrote his epistle shortly before his fateful sea-voyage); in this and other respects Drayton's villains resemble their counterparts on the Elizabethan stage—that is, those having a common origin in the Mortimer of *Edward II.* But there is an important difference.

This is revealed in the contrast between Marlowe's and Drayton's handling of the death of Mortimer. In *Edward II* the heroic villain stands revealed at the end as the slave of Fortune, though there is nothing servile about the way he faces death. Drayton's Mortimer, though also heroic in the face of death, does not call on Fortune in his last hour; instead, he identifies himself with Caesar ("Thus Caesar died, and thus dies Mortimer"), and justifiably so, since like Caesar he is an over-reacher paying the price demanded of one who sets imperial ambitions over love of country. Marlowe's Mortimer falls because his aspirations are without limit, and to Marlowe there is something splendid about this. In Drayton's version of the story, Mortimer's great sin is a failure in patriotism. This is revealed to us much earlier in the poem when he suffers neither anxiety nor physical discomfort in his exile in France, because "To Mortimer all countries are his own." It is appropriate, Drayton says, that the young Earl is banished to the Continent, "Which being boundless, honor hath no bound."

Drayton is less clear on what we are to think about Queen Isabel. Her adultery is not condoned, but it is understood, as is her revenge wish (some deliberate parallels with Medea are made). Curiously, at the end of the poem she curses her son, then settles down to a life of repentance, an incongruity corrected in *The Barons' Wars*, where Drayton had become sufficiently disparaging of her to omit any mention of repentance. In both versions, though, she shares Mortimer's Marlovian ambivalence (a quality recognized by Jonson, who described the actions of the poem as "valiant crimes") :[17] we are supposed to be attracted to her at first out of sympathy for her unfortunate marriage, but when, by the final canto, she has turned against her family as well as her country, she becomes a microcosm of the unnatural strife that has engulfed all England. Seen thus, she is a fit partner in Mortimer's self-aggrandizement, though one wishes she were as consistent a character in the rest of the poem as she is in the last canto.

Like other Elizabethan narrative poets, of course, Drayton is not nearly so concerned with character as with meaning. His poetic imagination is brought to bear fully on the depiction of the atrocities that his characters, and the types which they represent, bring into the land:

> The mangled bodies diving in the stream,
> Now up, now down, like tumbling porpoise swim,
> The water cover'd with a bloody cream,
> To the beholder horrible and grim:
> Here lies a head, and there doth lie a limb,
> Which in the sands the swelling waters souse,
> That all the shores seem like a slaughter-house. (ll. 435–41)

The battle scene from which this stanza is taken is replete with the charnel-house imagery of "slimy seggs," "bowels, arms, and legs," "carcasses . . . heaped like a wall," and "senseless steel." It is clearly not a gratuitous description, but a calculated effort to instill terror into the reader—to prepare him to accept the grisly *sententia* which concludes it: "Such is the horror of these civil broils, / When with our blood we fat our native soils" (ll. 447–48). In his pre-Machiavellian naïvety, Drayton sees politics as an extension of moral issues. To him, as to medieval men, all public evils are ultimately adduceable to *Superbia*: pride of over-reachers, factional men, and usurpers.

A word must be said about the customary view that *The Barons' Wars* is a notable improvement on *Mortimeriados*.[18] The advantage of the latter version is, as has been pointed out, the strengthening of the narrative structure. Two disadvantages, however, remain more significant: one is Drayton's mishandling of the ottava rima, another is the often pedantic determination to show off his scholarship. In both areas we can see the malignant (at least for Drayton) influence of Samuel Daniel's *Civil Wars*. Just as he was misled into following Chapman with *Endimion and Phoebe*, he erred in trying to emulate Daniel by "modernizing" a poem that had been better left untouched. Space does not allow a lengthy defense of this view, nor does common sense demand it. Let a few instances suffice.

In the matter of his showing off his erudition, we may compare the events beginning Canto IV of *The Barons' Wars* (ll. 1–184) with the parallel section in *Mortimeriados* (ll. 1296–1351). The revised version is almost four times as long, chiefly because Drayton has added new material (in lines 9–120) concerning the treason of Sir Andrew Herckley, who conspired with the Scots against the throne; the arrest of Torlton Bishop of Hereford; and the causes, wholly of Drayton's own framing, behind the Earl of Kent's joining with Queen Isabel. None of this is to be found in *Mortimeriados*, nor is it necessary for an understanding of the action. Other changes in this passage of *The Barons' Wars* also arise from a wish to make the poem more "historical." In *Mortimeriados* passing reference is made to Isabel's meeting with Henry, Earl of Lancaster, at her landing: "England's Earl-marshal, Lord of all that coast, / With bells and bonfires welcomes her to shore" (ll. 1345–46). In *The Barons' Wars* the new account is not only detailed beyond reason, it is a grammatical nightmare:

> When Henry, Brother to that luckless Prince,
> The first great mover of that civil strife,
> Thomas, whom Law but lately did convince,
> That had at Pomfret left his wretched life;

> That Henry, in whose bosom ever since
> Revenge lay covered, watching for relief,
> Like fire in some fat mineral of the Earth,
> Finding a fit vent, gives her furie birth.

> And being Earl Marshal, great upon that coast,
> With bells and bonfires welcomes her ashore;
> And by his office gath'ring up an host,
> Shew'd the great spleen that he to Edward bore,
> Nor of the same, abash'd at all to boast;
> The Clergy's power in readiness before,
> And on their friends a tax as freely laid,
> To raise munition for their present aid. (IV.22, 23)

The diffuseness of these lines brings up the second problem in Drayton's revision, the stanza. The use of ottava rima makes us suspect Daniel's influence, especially when Drayton himself admits in his preface that "all stanzas are in my opinion but tyrants and torturers, when they make invention obey their number." Particularly when he had achieved such success with the heroic couplet in the *Epistles*, it is hard to see any reason in his choice of the new stanza beyond the rather shallow one of imitating Daniel.[19] His tendency in revising is really to pad the old seven-line stanza with an eighth line, which neither adds to nor subtracts from the original sense. The reproach to London in *Mortimeriados*,

> Thy channels serve for ink, for paper stones,
> And on the ground, write murthers, incests, rapes,
> And for thy pens, a heap of dead-men's bones,
> Thy letters, ugly forms, and monstrous shapes;
> And when the earth's great hollow concave gapes,
> Then sink them down, lest she we live upon
> Do leave our use, and fly subjection. (ll. 1541–47)

becomes, in *The Barons' Wars*,

> Her channel serv'd for ink, her paper, stones,
> Whereon to write her murther, incest, rape;
> And for her pen's, a heap of dead men's bones,
> To make each letter in some monstrous shape;
> And for her accents, sad departing groans:
> And that to time no desp'rate act should scape,

If she with pride again should be o'ergone,
To take that book, and sadly look thereon. (IV.45)

In the second version, a logically unnecessary fifth line has been added to the scribal metaphor, just at the point where the third "a" rhyme interposes to change the rhyme royal to ottava rima. Such "revision" takes little more than a facility for rhyming. It is as if the poet simply hunted for a rhyme-word and built a line around it. Other instances of this practice might be given.[20]

Regardless of stylistic differences, both versions are deeply impressed with the stamp of monumental history: pursuit of greatness, idealization or romanticizing of the past, and reproach of the present for failing to learn the lessons of the past. Like *Mortimeriados*, *The Barons' Wars* repeatedly calls attention to the standard pattern followed by political intrigue and abuse, whether past or present.

In Canto IV of *The Barons' Wars* Drayton compares the fall of King Edward's friends with that of a building, after a "large pillar, of a Lordly height" (i.e., Edward) has been removed. The commentary on Edward's fall is an admonition in the vein of *The Mirror for Magistrates*, and not the author's airing of some personal grievance (Drayton's quest for patronage had not yet taken him into the penetralia of the Court). It condemns two general classes of politicians: princes or great men who abuse their rank, especially by "Promoting whom they please, not whom they should," and parasites or "minions" (as Drayton and fellow critics of Court favoritism were fond of calling them)—officers who usurp the places of "men of merit" by flattery and catering to their masters' vices. The overthrow of men like Edward is thus not effected by their enemies, but is "Procur'd by those whom fondly they preferr'd." The commentary ends with a couplet less in the tradition of Baldwin and his followers than in the witty, aphoristic spirit of the Restoration, indicating, I think, that Drayton is an important link in the evolution of English political verse from *The Mirror* to *Absalom and Achitophel*: "For great wits forged into factious tools / Prove great men (oft) to be the greatest fools" (IV.63).

Following the lead of other poet-historians, especially dramatists, Drayton reviled in particular those favorites who took advantage of weak superiors. *Woodstock* and *Richard II* both reflect the evils of favoritism in the court of an intemperate monarch. In 2 *Henry VI* the commoners rise up not against the King, as their spokesmen take pains to declare, but against Suffolk and his worthless retainers. The hero of *Bussy D'Ambois*, in which the King is always treated with respectful neutrality, is especially hard on "great men" who use the King, like the Duke of Guise. "Show me a great man," he says in a long harangue,

> That rules so much more than his suffering king,
> That he makes kings of his subordinate slaves: . . .
> I'll play the vulture, and so thump his liver,
> That, like a huge unlading Argosy,
> He shall confess all, and you then may hang him. (III.2)

Again and again, the accused enemies of political order in Elizabethan and Jacobean literature are those who take advantage of a lenient monarch—whether they be over-reaching nobility (like Mortimer) or self-serving, clever nobodies (like Bushy and Greene or Piers Gaveston). Nor was this resentment a mere fictional convention: during the stormy parliament of 1620, when some of the most powerful lords complained to James of the boldness of the House of Commons, a member who was there replied that "they best defended the King's prerogative who tried to preserve it against the vermin that would destroy the commonwealth."[21]

Drayton probably had something more specific in mind than these general classes when in 1602 he wrote the admonitory comments on Edward II's fall. The Earl of Essex and his party might justly have been censured for "Promoting whom they please," since their lavish distribution of honors, even knighthoods, was a general scandal.[22] Equally germane to contemporary problems is Drayton's reference to a fall "Procur'd by those whom fondly they preferr'd." Now this cannot logically relate to the events of Drayton's narrative, since Edward's fall is "procured" by Mortimer—hardly a royal favorite. The lines fit in well with Essex's situation in 1601, however, in that his fall was popularly thought to have been procured by several of his former protégés, most notably Francis Bacon.

It was probably the potential for contemporary relevance in the story of Edward II that prevented Sir Francis Hubert's *Deplorable Life and Death of Edward the Second* from being licensed for publi-

cation in Elizabeth's last years. Hubert's distrust of those who have
the ruler's ear echoes that of Drayton and other historical poets:

> For [the King] himself is blameless oft (God knows),
> Except it be because he does not know
> The noted scandals that arise from those
> On whom he doth his favors most bestow,
> Which they abusing, discontents may grow
> Against the Prince, though not deserving them:
> So apt we are, even goodness to condemn.[23]

In Hubert's poem, Edward once more exemplifies the careless ruler
who allows his favorites to make havoc of the kingdom. The revival
of this old poem in 1628, just when the Duke of Buckingham's
power had reached its critical state, may have been coincidental, but
if so it was fortunate, for Buckingham and Essex alike represent a
familiar type in the historical patterns of the Tudor and Stuart age.[24]

England's Heroical Epistles

As monumental history, Drayton's two poems on Mortimer are
flawed only by the absence of a positive sense of national destiny,
perhaps understandable in view of his admonitory purpose. Other
poetry written about this time, however, maintains his belief that
England, from her very beginnings, had a leading place in the divine
plan. In Song XI of *Poly-Olbion*, when the Muse has left Wales for
the first sojourn into England, there is an elegiac pause while the
Weaver River looks back on the ruins of Celtic greatness. Only the
ways of Providence can explain the withdrawal of Arthur's race
from preeminence: "Needs must they fall, whom heaven doth to
destruction haste" (XI.160). In the new Saxon race we are meant to
see foreshadowings of the bravery and aggressiveness that would
make England an international power:

> The noble Saxons were a Nation hard and strong,
> On sundry Lands and Seas, in warfare nuzzled long;
> Affliction throughly knew; and in proud Fortune's spite,
> Even in the jaws of Death had dar'd her utmost might.
> (XI.179–82)

This belief that England is foreordained to greatness among countries finds expression in much of Drayton's historical poetry, but nowhere is it more firmly enunciated than in *England's Heroical Epistles*.

The literary origins of these twenty-four verse letters may lead us to place undue emphasis on the love stories they entail, and to overlook their mainly political purpose. These origins are threefold: Ovid's *Heroides*, the "tragedies" of the *Mirror for Magistrates*, and the set speech of the contemporary theater. In the Ovidian models, where the preference is always for loving over fighting, patriotism and politics certainly have no place. Unlike Ovid, Drayton has assembled a cast of historical figures who were deeply embroiled in the destiny of their country, and in almost all cases he has turned our eyes to the political events surrounding the lovers rather than to their private passions.[25] The contemporary stage monologue influenced the style of the *Epistles* considerably, but as every reader of history plays knows, the monologue was used as often to explain the political situation as to reveal the inner conflicts of the speaker. The influence of the *Mirror* comes mainly through Daniel's *Rosamond*, the probable inspiration for the *Epistles*, rather than the original works of Baldwin's generation. In Drayton's poems Providence plays the role that belonged to Fortune in the *Mirror*. And if Drayton recounts the falls of some of his illustrious men, he has also fertilized the barren political philosophy of the *Mirror* poets. As Tillyard observes, "There is nothing at all in the *Mirror* of Hall's master theme, the working out of destiny over the stretch of history from Richard II to the Tudors."[26] Whether Drayton took it from Hall or not is difficult to say, but this same theme, which he is the first to merge with the conventional ideas of the *Mirror*, accounts for the design of his *Heroical Epistles*.

To one who reads through these poems in sequence the political design is not at first evident. One reason for this, I believe, is that the first two pairs of epistles were written before a plan ever suggested itself, for the letters of King John and Matilda certainly bear evidence of early composition. There is, for example, the "Simpsonian rhyme" (as C. S. Lewis calls it) of Matilda's, "Mildness would better suit with majesty, / Than rash revenge and rough severity" (ll. 119–20), and John's, "Lest that their seed, mark'd with deformity, / Should be a blemish to posterity" (ll. 117–18). The proportion of feminine rhymes is far higher in these epistles than in the others,[27] and the contrived language of some of Drayton's earliest sonnets is recalled in such lines as the following in the letter of King John:

> You blusht, I blusht; your cheek pale, pale was mine,
> My red, thy red, my whiteness answered thine;
> You sigh'd, I sigh'd, we both one passion prove,
> But thy sigh is for hate, my sigh for love. (ll. 15–18)

All indications are that Drayton began the *Epistles* in imitation of *Rosamond*, intending to write only the letters of King John and Matilda, and as so often happens in the act of composition, discovered in the form possibilities that had hitherto not been imagined.

The political issues are first broached in the epistles of Queen Isabel and Mortimer, and from then on they are of paramount concern to the "heroical" writers. In Mortimer's epistle we catch Drayton as a monumental historian in his first coloring of fact, as the Earl describes his parentage:

> My grandsire was the first, since Arthur's reign,
> That the Round Table rectified again:
> To whose great court at Kenilworth did come
> The peerless knighthood of all Christendom;
> Whose princely order honor'd England more
> Than all the conquests she achiev'd before. (ll. 53–58)

The association of Mortimer with Arthur is intended to cast a patriotic aura round Mortimer's ensuing war, almost as if to say that the spirit of Arthur is guiding England, through this ill-fated hero, back on the true course by ridding her of a weak and irresponsible ruler. We can appreciate Drayton's coloring when we compare his passage on the deeds of Mortimer's grandfather with its source in Stow's *Annals*: "The worthy soldier, Roger Mortimer, at Killingworth, appointed a knightly game, which was called the Round Table, of 100 knights and so many Ladies, to the which, for the exercise of arms, there came many warlike knights from divers kingdoms." To Stow the Round Table is a "game," while Drayton has made it a knightly order, having removed it from Killingworth to the more romantic Kenilworth. All of this history-becoming-romance is

owing, of course, to the Arthurian mystique initially fostered by
official Tudor propaganda, then by patriotic Englishmen like Drayton, for whom it became part of the social mythology.[28]

The general plan of the *Heroical Epistles*, at least from Mortimer and Isabel on, is to show divine Providence guiding England
through a troublesome past into a glorious present under Elizabeth.
"Heroic" men and women, as Drayton defines them, are especially
fit to execute the will of God; they in fact "for greatness of mind
come near to gods," in that they have "a great and mighty spirit, far
above the earthly weakness of men."[29] In imposing his providential
design on the epistles, Drayton has divided them into three equal
groups: one describing attempted seductions by royal figures (Henry
II, John, Edward the Black Prince, Edward IV), another concerning
liaisons between a queen and a nobleman (Isabel and Mortimer,
Katherine and Owen Tudor, Margaret and Suffolk, Mary and
Charles Brandon), a third containing faithful lovers' consolations
(Richard II and Isabel, Duke Humphrey and Elinor Cobham, Surrey and Geraldine, Jane Gray and Dudley). The arrangement of
the three groups within the work maintains a sense of variety, yet
there is an awareness of gradual development among the parts. As
if in tableau, the characters progress from the self-centered Plantagenet monarchs Henry and John (in the seduction group) to the
selfless patriots Surrey and Jane Gray (in the consolation group).
The central four pairs introduce the great crisis of English history
—at least as it was presented on the contemporary stage—Richard's
deposition, Duke Humphrey's betrayal, and the disintegrating influence of Margaret and Suffolk.

Some of the love affairs are deliberately portrayed so as to point
the way to Tudor greatness. The epistles of Katherine and Owen
Tudor introduce a ray of hope at the hour of greatest darkness.
Katherine warmly commends Tudor's Welsh lineage, his "royal
consanguinity" with "Pendragon's race," and she incidentally anticipates Henry VII's claims to the throne by rehearsing her own royal
genealogy.[30] In reply, Tudor claims descent from "great Cadwalla-
der," last king of the "ancient Race of Trojans"—as Drayton tells
us. Almost certainly, Drayton firmly believed the Tudor claim. If
he had intended merely to present a series of great love affairs in
these epistles, the natural choice of a mate for Katherine would have

been Henry V, not Tudor. The wooing of Katherine was a well-known event in popular historical literature, as witness *Henry V* and *The Famous Victories*. In Owen Tudor, however, Drayton saw a means not only to foreshadow the resurgence of England under the Tudors, but to link up his country's legendary past with her real present. This was a match made in heaven, with an eye to England's future. As Tudor says,

> Then cast no future doubts, nor fear no hate,
> When it so long hath been foretold by fate,
> And by the all-disposing doom of Heav'n,
> Before our births, we to one bed were giv'n.[31]

Surrey, the poet and chivalric hero of popular fiction, represents another aspect of England's emergent greatness—her entry into the mainstream of Renaissance culture. In Rotterdam, Surrey reports that he has "made a minute of a winter's night" with Erasmus and More; in Germany he dabbles in magic with Cornelius Agrippa. The climax of his grand tour, the joust at Florence, symbolizes the competitive spirit between Renaissance culture in England and on the Continent, an idea later given voice by Surrey himself:

> I find no cause, nor judge I reason why,
> My Country should give place to Lombardy;
> As goodly flow'rs on Thamesis do grow,
> As beautify the banks of wanton Po;
> As many Nymphs as haunt rich Arnus' strand,
> By silver Severn tripping hand in hand. (ll. 227–32)

Geraldine replies with some unkind words for those Englishmen who, unlike her lover,

> travel hence, t'enrich their minds with skill,
> Leave here their good, and bring home others' ill;
> Which seem to like all countries but their own,
> Affecting most where they the least are known;
> Their leg, their thigh, their back, their neck, their head,
> As they had been in sev'ral countries bred;
> In their attire, their gesture, and their gait,
> Found in each one, in all, Italianate;
> So well in all deformity in fashion,
> Borrowing a limb of ev'ry sev'ral Nation;

> And nothing more than England hold in scorn,
> So live as strangers whereas they were born. (ll. 119–30)

Geraldine's is one of the most frequently repeated themes of the age
—from Ascham's *Schoolmaster* to Jonson's *Volpone*: the danger that
Continental viciousness will corrupt the pristine purity of the English race.

The story of Jane Gray, the popular martyr in the cause of
English Protestantism, is too well known to need retelling here. Her
consolation to Guildford Dudley implies reassurance for all Elizabethans of the unerring Providence of God:

> Yet Heav'n forbid that Mary's womb should bring
> England's fair scepter to a foreign king;
> But she to fair Elizabeth shall leave it,
> Which broken, hurt, and wounded shall receive it:
> And on her temples having plac'd the crown,
> Root out the dregs Idolatry hath sown;
> And Sion's glory shall again restore,
> Laid ruin, waste, and desolate before;
> And from black cinders and rude heaps of stones,
> Shall gather up the martyrs' sacred bones;
> And shall extirp the power of Rome again,
> And cast aside the heavy yoke of Spain.[32] (ll. 171–82)

In the couplet that brings all the *Heroical Epistles* to a close Drayton
has Guildford Dudley repeat his wife's auspicious theme: "And
when we shall so happily be gone, / Leave it to heaven to give the
rightful throne."

In general outlines, then, the *Heroical Epistles* convey an optimism and faith in the nation that is typical of the spirit of the 1590s,
even though this decade was rapidly discovering new anxieties, especially over the future of the throne. But Drayton's eye is usually
on the future as well as the past, and it is probably in view of the
future that he includes the epistles of Queen Mary and Charles
Brandon.

The story of these lovers has inherent romantic interest. Mary,
daughter of Henry VII, a beautiful and talented girl, was pledged in
marriage to the aging French King Louis XII. When the old King
died only a few months after the wedding, Henry VIII sent an
English escort to bring his sister home. Leading this escort was

Charles Brandon, Duke of Suffolk, who according to some had already caught Mary's eye. They were secretly married in France, then publicly married on their return to England, much to the displeasure of Henry. There they retired to the Suffolk estate and by all accounts lived happily ever after.

It is a charming story in its own right; however, this marriage held considerable implications for the most sensitive political question in Drayton's time, that of the royal succession. Aside from James VI of Scotland, in the opinion of a contemporary, there were eleven "competitors that gape for the death of that good old Princess the now Queen."[33] If James was ineligible—as some said he must be since he was a foreigner by birth—the next claimant was Arabella Stuart, whose right was thwarted by her father's illegitimacy. After Arabella there were a good many who had some remote claim to the crown: the earls of Huntington, Westmoreland, and Derby, even some foreigners, like the King of Spain or the Infanta—a favorite choice with Catholics like Robert Parsons. One of the less fanciful claimants, however, was Edward Seymour, son of Catherine Seymour and Edward, Earl of Hertford, whose great-grandparents were Mary and Charles Brandon. A glance at this segment of the Seymour genealogy will show why a patriotic Englishman might well prefer this native candidate to the King of Scotland:

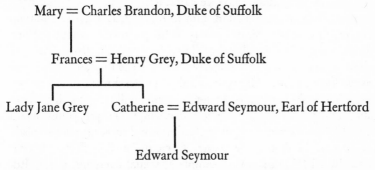

Mary = Charles Brandon, Duke of Suffolk

Frances = Henry Grey, Duke of Suffolk

Lady Jane Grey   Catherine = Edward Seymour, Earl of Hertford

Edward Seymour

Elizabeth dismissed this claim on two counts: first, Catherine and Edward Seymour were not legitimately married, for by an act of 1536 persons of royal blood were forbidden to marry without the sovereign's consent; second, Brandon already had a wife when he married into the royal family, so that all his line was illegitimate.

The second point is important regarding Drayton's epistles, for although the charge of Brandon's bigamy was well known at the time, it goes unmentioned by Drayton.[34]

We can only speculate on the reasons for Drayton's (admittedly unproven) partisanship. Did he know of the support Ralegh and Cecil were reputed to have given the Seymour heir, and was he trying for their good graces? At any rate, Drayton's honoring the Brandon romance would not have endeared him to Elizabeth, and may even have brought him some sort of rebuff during the last years of her reign.[35] It does, however, seem reasonable to infer from these epistles, especially in the light of Drayton's other historical poetry, that his loyalties were to country before crown, and that he would have preferred a thoroughly English, thoroughly Protestant king to a foreigner who had already shown a certain weakness in managing the affairs of his own nation. Charles Brandon's father, after all, had been standard-bearer to Henry VII at Bosworth Field, while James VI's mother had lived for the overthrow of true religion in England.

As with the epistles of Mary and Charles Brandon, so with the other pairs: the private, personal elements of the love story are given, but subserve the dominant public and historical theme. If the guiding force in the whole work is Providence, the chief agent of Providence is the power of love and beauty. Owen Tudor (ll. 152–28) describes his propitious romance as brought on by a "celestial fire," Katherine's beauty compelling him to marry her. Charles Brandon is as much taken by Mary's beauty as by her royal lineage: "When Heav'n's lamp shines, all other lights be lost" (ll. 166). The less admirable characters in the epistles are often led by an ignoble, excessive form of love: Henry II's adulterous attachment to Rosamond is seen (ll. 49–74) as that of an aging failure, willing to sacrifice reputation and family for a pathetic last attempt "To put young blood into old Aeson's veins." Robert Burton found in King John's epistle evidence of the destructive power of love melancholy.[36] The lascivious Edward IV is made an example of sexual irresponsibility: "Edward's intemperate desires," reads Drayton's gloss, "with which he was wholly overcome, how tragically they in his offspring were punished, is universally known. A Mirror, representing their oversight that leave their children what to possess than what to imitate."[37]

With this pervasive theme of love as it advances or deters man's capacity for the heroic—that is, for acting in the cause of England—the *Epistles* are a counterpart to the middle books of *The Faerie Queen*, where the providential role of love is a central motif, especially the role of love as an adjunct to virtue. Spenser hails love as a god:

> The fatal purpose of divine foresight
> Thou doest effect in destined descents,
> Through deep impression of thy secret might,
> And stirredst up th' heroes' high intents,
> Which the late world admires for wondrous monuments. (III.3.2)

Once again Drayton translates a Spenserian theme from the mythic to the actual, as the personae of his epistles occupy historical roles of which Spenser presents the types. Spenser's noble figures, in whom love and virtue are (or become) perfectly complementary, like Arthur and Britomart, correspond in Drayton to Queen Katherine or Lady Jane Gray. The tormented and melancholy Scudamour might be compared to Mortimer's Isabel or to Richard II, while the clever, ignoble Paridel finds his match in Edward IV. Each of Drayton's heroes provides a study of the role of love in the heroic life, an issue that was especially fruitful in English literature from Sidney's *Arcadia* to the heroic plays of Dryden.[38] In both the *Heroical Epistles* and *The Barons' Wars* the perversion of the heroic, active life is accompanied by pride and illicit love; the result is disorder in society. Thus the greater the focus on self rather than on the public welfare, the less constructive the role of the character in shaping English fortunes.

The universality of Drayton's theme of heroic love is reinforced by several explicit comparisons of his characters with figures from classical mythology: Queen Mary and Charles Brandon are Hero and Leander, Edward and Jane Shore are Paris and Helen, Geraldine and Surrey are Penelope and Ulysses. Such parallels also serve to remind the reader that the genre of this work is, after all, a classical one, and Drayton would seem to be inviting comparison with Ovid's *Heroides*. In this regard, it may at least be said that by unifying his epistles around the single theme of national destiny guided by heroic love, Drayton has produced a more coherent set of poems than Ovid.[39] England, the implied subject of every letter, acquires an almost personal dimension, as it does in that more ambitious work, well under way by 1597, *Poly-Olbion*, where England is a vast terrestrial spirit, "Which livedst long before the all-earth-drowning flood, / Whilst yet the world did swarm with her gigantic brood" (I.9–10). That poem also shares with the *Epistles* and other works of Drayton's, such as the 1606 *Odes* and the Lucanesque *Barons' Wars*,[40] the objective of rivaling the ancients, reminding us that Drayton's classicism was that of national-minded Renaissance poets everywhere, from the Pleiade, in their quest for a long French poem, to Tasso and Milton.

Of equal importance with Ovid is the influence of the contemporary theater, for Drayton's familiarity with the stage (if not, by this time, his actual experience as a playwright) effected a greater flexibility in his language and a loosening of syntax—a characteristic that I have earlier noted in his revised sonnets of 1599. By comparison with the early legends, the *Epistles* also show that Drayton had learned something about the dramatist's technique of characterization. They may not be "dramatic monologues" in the received sense,[41] but they partake of the dramatist's authorial distance, in that even Machiavellians like Margaret and Suffolk are portrayed with an insidious sympathy reminiscent of Marlowe. At times, as in the letters of Mortimer, Queen Isabel, and Edward IV, it is difficult to know where the poet stands without resorting to his gloss or to other evidence external to the text. Such treatment befits these characters, however, for in their misplaced confidence they reflect perfectly the ironic predicament of malevolent power in a providential universe, unwittingly furthering the very cause they seek to overthrow.

The Legend of Great Cromwell

Something has already been said of Drayton's "legend" *Peirs Gaveston*; its successor, *Matilda*, is written in much the same windily didactic vein. The third legend, *Robert Duke of Normandy* (entered November 1596), though unimportant as poetry, is a small landmark in Drayton's career, since it signals a turning away from the ornate style of the earlier legends, and points toward the middle style of the *Heroical Epistles* and later work. Frustrated in his attempts to keep up in the rarified Ovidian atmosphere of Lodge, Chapman, Marlowe, and Shakespeare, Drayton fell back into the path that best suited his conservative temperament, for *Robert* is a medieval vision-poem, reminiscent of Baldwin and Lydgate in its account of Robert's rise and fall at the hands of the allegorical Ladies Fame and Fortune. It is far too long (1,421 lines), however, and it confirms C. S. Lewis' warning "to expect the worst from any descendant of *The Mirror for Magistrates*."[42]

The last of these legends, *The Legend of Great Cromwell*, provides an unusually objective treatment of a still controversial character, which has led some to the belief that Drayton was following Daniel's lead as a historian who demanded absolute fidelity to the facts. It is true, as one writer has said, that Drayton's opinions about Cromwell "are neither consistently maintained nor very clearly expressed,"[43] calling to mind similar problems with the portrayal of Gaveston and Queen Isabel. Yet it is also true that this poem avoids the sententious moralizing that makes the early legends and so many earlier *Mirror* poems unreadable.

In this poem we come to know Cromwell through his own words and actions, rather than through any imperatives of the author. Only one remark by Drayton tips us off to his own view, in his preface to the four *Legends*:

> Last of all, in Cromwell thou hast the example of a new man's fortune, made great by arts of court, and reach of a shrewd wit, upon the advantages of a corrupt prince and times; showing that nothing is certain in newness, where the creature's fall may in some measure deliver the mortal creator from the envy of his proper acts and insolencies [i.e., things unaccustomed (because new)].

These words are doubly important, for they not only help us toward an understanding of Drayton's intentions; they also point out the manifest bearing of the poem on contemporary events. Like *Mortimeriados* and the *Heroical Epistles, Cromwell* presents the reader of 1607 with problems familiar in his own time—namely those surrounding the man of new fortunes who is permitted to rise at the whim of an extravagant monarch in a corrupt, ambition-ridden court. Spenser's most succinct presentation of this theme is in the Court of Philotime (*Faerie Queen* II.vii.43–50), which allegorizes the Court vices of ambition, flattery, and envy. Drayton, seeking to condemn the same vices, typically chooses to render them in a "real," historical court.

Cromwell's rise is all the more suspect, at least from a Country point of view, in that his first steps are taken up the ladder of commerce, as a merchant's secretary in Antwerp, then as a petitioner at Rome for the economic interests of Boston. His own words also betray him as the very apostle of newfangleness:

> You that but boast your ancestors' proud style,
> And the large stem whence your vain greatness grew,
> When you yourselves are ignorant and vile,
> Nor glorious thing dare actually pursue,
> That all good spirits would utterly exile,
> Doubting their worth should else discover you,
> Giving yourselves unto ignoble things;
> Base I proclaim you, though deriv'd from Kings. (ll. 121–28)

It is an attractive argument, but specious. Somewhat more damning is the Machiavellian way in which Cromwell uses people:

> In foreign parts near friends I yet forsake,
> That had before been deeply bound to me,
> And would again I use of them should make,
> But still my stars command I should be free. (ll. 241–44)

Of course all of this scheming gets Cromwell into high office, but it also earns him a trip to the block. The concluding stanzas point the moral, and the implied values are typically Elizabethan—first the warning against self-serving and the extravagant use of wealth:

> Self-loving man, what sooner doth abuse,
> And more than his prosperity doth wound?
> Into the deep but fall, how can he choose,
> That over-strides whereon his foot to ground?
> Who sparingly prosperity doth use,
> And to himself doth after-ill propound,
> Unto his height who happily doth climb,
> Sits above Fortune, and controlleth Time. (ll. 937–44)

Then a warning against flatterers and usurpers:

But whil'st we strive too suddenly to rise
By flatt'ring Princes with a servile tongue,
And being soothers to their tyrannies,
Work our much woes by what doth many wrong,
And unto others tending injuries,
Unto ourselves it hapning oft among.
In our own snares unluckily are caught,
Whil'st our attempts fall instantly to naught. (ll. 953–60)

The focus upon ambition and the vice of novelty obliged Drayton to represent in a somewhat untraditional or un-Protestant light Cromwell's suppression of the monasteries; this has led readers to the erroneous belief that Drayton was sympathetic with Roman Catholicism.[44] Such readers overlook the very great irony that Drayton must have seen in the confrontation between Cromwell and the Catholics: the irony by which a decadent institution, festering with worldliness, pride, deceit, and ambition, should be toppled by a man who shared the same qualities. When Cromwell visits the pope, he sees Rome as "the great school of the false world," and it is easy to see why he fares so well among kindred spirits. The long paraphrase from *Piers Plowman* (B-Text, passus XX—Drayton was one of many who thought *Piers Plowman* a Reformation poem) on the friar's subversion of conscience is intended to reflect the state of all Catholicism at that time. The "new" fashion of easy-penance-for-a-price endows the friars with great success, financial if not pastoral. However, even while these self-serving men undermine the foundations of religion, they are themselves being supplanted by a new order of self-serving under Cromwell. It is part of the eternal cycle of evil feeding upon itself, every revolution of which leaves the noble institutions of the past—primitive English Christianity included—more enfeebled and impoverished. Drayton's voice seems elegiac, drained of the exuberance of the 1590s, as he surveys the history of the church in the light of Henry VIII's reign:

The wisest and most provident but build
For Time again but only to destroy,
The costly piles and monuments we gild,
Succeeding Time shall reckon but a toy,
Vicissitude impartially will'd,
The goodliest things be subject to annoy,

> And what one age did studiously maintain,
> The next again accounteth vile and vain. (ll. 753–60)

We sense here, of course, a Spenserian nostalgia for the venerable ways of an earlier Christianity, but we can hardly infer from this that Drayton sympathized with Rome, any more than we can label Spenser a papist because he does not condone the sacrilege of the Blatant Beast. In the same way, while Drayton's poem on the whole condemns Cromwell, it manages to convey a sense of admiration, even wonder, akin to that of Milton for Satan. Cromwell is the epitome of Hobbesian man, competitive, selfish, driven by insatiable greed; by a peculiar kind of travesty, he is also the Renaissance man, a Bussy D'Ambois—soldier of fortune and shrewd courtier of boundless energy and imagination. Cromwell tells us that in his humble childhood he already harbored a secret "glorious fire," which the "dull purblind ignorance" of ordinary men could not see. His pride and sense of destiny are one with Mortimer's and with the feelings of all strong men, real or fictitious, who thrilled the Renaissance imagination. More than anything else, the lure of power and the school of fame set the English Renaissance apart from the Continental. The ideal of *virtù* had its great patron in Machiavelli, but some of its greatest practitioners were Elizabethan Englishmen.[45] And in that age of patriotism the nation as a whole acquired a Cromwellian lust for power and eminence, transcending the ambitions of any particular men. There was more of England in the character of Cromwell than Drayton or any of his readers realized.

It would be some twenty years before Drayton would continue, in his *Battle of Agincourt*, the study of the relationship between national destiny and the individual human spirit. In the interim he published almost no new poetry except *Poly-Olbion*. That work in itself was enough to occupy much of his time, but one senses a deeper explanation for this unproductiveness: a contempt bordering on despair for the sins of his age. I have in part accounted for this later melancholy in the first chapter, though a fuller discussion of it must accompany that on Drayton's satire. Suffice it to say that the 1607 *Cromwell* marks an end for the time being to Drayton's activity as a historical poet, except for the excursions into history in *Poly-Olbion*, where this incipient hostility to his age manifests itself in a shift from monumentalism in the first part of the poem to bleak antiquarianism in the second.

3 | ANTIQUARIANISM AND RENEWAL

> So oft as I with state of present time
> The image of the antique world compare,
> When as mans age was in his freshest prime,
> And the first blossoms of fair virtue bare,
> Such odds I find twixt those, and these which are,
> As that, through long continuance of his course,
> Me seems the world is run quite out of square
> From the first point of his appointed source,
> And being once amiss, grows daily worse and worse.
>
> (Spenser, *Faerie Queen* V, prologue)

Poly-Olbion Early and Late

Poly-Olbion, a poem as much remarked upon as little read,[1] is often taken for a purely descriptive work. True, there is description enough; but the poem was written with a purpose, the grounds of which are nowhere more clearly or eloquently expressed than in the tenth song:

> But, in things past so long (for all the world) we are
> Like to a man embarqu't and travelling the deep:
> Who sailing by some hill, or promontory steep
> Which juts into the sea, with an amazed eye
> Beholds the cleeves thrust up into the lofty sky.
> And th' more that he doth look, the more it draws his sight;
> Now at the craggy front, then at the wondrous weight:
> But, from the passed shore still as the swelling sail

> (Thrust forward by the wind) the floating bark doth hail,
> The mighty giant-heap, so less and lesser still
> Appeareth to the eye, until the monstrous hill
> At length shows like a cloud; and further being cast
> Is out of kenning quite: So, of the ages past;
> Those things that in their age much to be wondered were,
> Still as wing-footed time them farther off doth bear,
> Do lessen every hour. (ll. 308–23)

The imagery of these lines hints at the latent skepticism in Drayton's view of past and present. The sea, the present, is an eternally shifting place for man; the rocks of the past should provide him with both a reference point for navigating, and a model for stability. Yet because man's position is eternally shifting, moving from the known past into the unknown future, the rocks themselves seem temporary, as they remain only momentarily in his sight. This idea can lead to two kinds of historical thinking: one which holds that the historian must draw man back into the past, clearing away the mists of time —figuratively, keeping man in plain view of the rocks—and showing him the greatness that has been his. This is essentially the position of the monumental historian, and it is the prevailing one in the first part of *Poly-Olbion*. The dominant view in the second part of the poem, published ten years later, is antiquarian: the only valid reality lies in the past, and the historian's office is to anchor his life perpetually upon the rocks, so that he may know truth rather than the ephemera of the present and future, which would otherwise engulf him.

In the first part of *Poly-Olbion*, the antiquarian voice is audible though muffled. For Drayton, the refusal of Englishmen to accept their legendary history, to tolerate the few distortions of fact that accompany it, represents a crass devaluation of tradition. The Wye River, in a long speech on this subject, says:

> Here then I cannot choose but bitterly exclaim
> Against those fools that all Antiquity defame,
> Because they have found out some credulous ages laid
> Slight fictions with the truth.

She inveighs against "critics,"

> . . . whose judgements are so strict;
> And he the bravest man who most can contradict

> That which decrepit Age (which forced is to lean
> Upon Tradition) tells.

The Dee River's speech constitutes a further apology for tradition. Praising the ancient Druids for their preservation of history in memory rather than by writing, she says that once men have committed a great deed to memory,

> They leave it their next Age, that leaves it hers again;
> So strongly which (me thinks) doth for Tradition make,
> As if you from the world it altogether take,
> You utterly subvert Antiquity thereby.

This reverence for the memorial past in an age of radical change naturally prompts abundant scorn for the present. The history of Brut has become a legend, "Which now the envious world doth slander for a dream." Even the reign of Arthur has been traduced by the present. In one of the many topographical myths of the poem, Drayton tells how the River Camel, where Arthur was taken after his last battle, now wanders distracted and aimless through the hallowed landscape:

> Even in the agedst face [she says] where beauty once did dwell,
> And nature (in the least) but seemed to excel,
> Time cannot make such waste, but something will appear,
> To show some little tract of delicacy there.
> Or some religious work, in building many a day,
> That this penurious age hath suffered to decay,
> Some limb or model, dragged out of the ruinous mass,
> The richness will declare in glory whilst it was:
> But Time upon my waste committed hath such theft,
> That of it Arthur here scarce memory hath left.

Drayton himself is less gentle than the Camel in his preface to Part I, where he writes a spirited denunciation of "this lunatic age," in which "the idle humorous world must hear of nothing that either savors of antiquity, or may awake it to seek after more than dull, slothtful ignorance may easily reach unto."[2]

Nevertheless, the first part of *Poly-Olbion* is not written merely out of reverence for the past. It has long been recognized that the poem is written in response to "the English desire for a national background no less noble than that of Troy and Rome, and to her conviction that her present rulers incarnated the ancient tradition."[3] Drayton inherits the defensiveness that seems to go along with new nationalism, and throughout the early songs of the poem I sense a desire to rehabilitate England in the eyes of the world. The Vale of Red Horse explains to the rest of the countryside that even though it is now neglected, poetry (Drayton's poetry) will revive its reputation:

> But when th'industrious Muse shall purchase me respect
> Of Countries near my site, and win me foreign fame
> (The Eden of you all deservedly that am)
> I shall as much be praised for delicacy then,
> As now in small account with vile and barbarous men.

If in the development of a society regional pride precedes national pride, *Poly-Olbion* represents the fusing of the two; for although the whole poem constitutes a monument to the English nation, Drayton has taken pains to extol the local attributes of all the shires. The same division of regional and national pride was glimpsed earlier in "An Ode Written in the Peak." Paradoxically—but the fact would seem historically necessary—regional topographical literature thrives toward the end of the nationalistic Tudor era, when poets who still retain their local pride are obliged to go to London for patronage, publishers, and an atmosphere congenial to their work.[4]

Other readers of *Poly-Olbion* have observed that one of the main structural devices in the poem is the repeated motif of rivalries and contentions, not only among the personified features of the landscape, but between the natural and historical wonders of England and those of classical antiquity.[5] Just as he had found English counterparts for Ovid's heroes in the *Epistles*, Drayton implies that for every Greek and Roman place or personage there is a corresponding one in his own country that is probably superior. The English naval heroes are called Argonauts (XIX.171), Maid Marian is the Diana of Sherwood Forest (XXVI.357), Guy of Warwick is the English Hercules (XIII.350), and the "most insatiate Danes," in their raids on coastal England, are likened to the Greeks invading Troy (XIII.374). In his wish to maintain this rivalry with the ancients, Drayton regrets the lack of a national Arthurian epic to surpass Homer's (III.404–8)—indicating some limits to his admiration for Spenser. Malvern Hill exclaims to Mount Olympus, "I envie not thy state, nor less myself do make" (VII.63). The curves and "crankling nookes" of the River Wye are said to be far more sinuous than those of the Meander (VII.197). Defending the historicity of Brut and other figures in Geoffrey of Monmouth's chronicle, Drayton asserts that these stories were not "idle tales . . . Nor fabulous, like those devised by the Greeks" (X.254–56).

How much of the second part of *Poly-Olbion* had already been composed by 1613 is uncertain. In a letter of 1619 to William Drummond, Drayton complained that the second part "lies by me; for the booksellers and I are in terms. They are a company of base knaves, whom I both scorn and kick at."[6] Undoubtedly the first part had not sold well, and Drayton should have thought himself lucky to find anyone willing to take on the expense of printing the last twelve songs. As late as 1624 the publishers of Part I were still trying to unload copies of the book, and not one of them cared to repeat his losses with the preparation of the second part in 1622.[7]

Anyone who has tried to keep pace with the vigorous Muse of Part I will feel at once the slackening in Part II. Was Drayton now simply carrying out a task in which he no longer had any interest? Had new publishers, or his new quasi-patron, Prince Charles, obliged him to make some unwanted changes? A recent commentator has offered an explanation that seems plausible to me because it sheds light on the question of Drayton's political and historical thought at this time. The change in the poem, he contends, is owing to a change in Drayton, who has lost confidence in the capacity of his age to imitate the past. Whereas in Part I he had hoped to inspire his countrymen by appealing to the beauty and history of England, in Part II the instruments of his appeal have become the sole objects of his attention, and he is no longer concerned with their ends. He sees himself as the last Elizabethan.[8]

In view of the evidence, it is scarcely questionable that by 1622 a profound change has taken place in the poet. The lively contention for supremacy in fame between the Anglo-Saxons and the Celts, which had dominated Part I, has disappeared. The whole poem has become more topographical, and its historical passages are more often simply descriptive chronicles. The newly published section opens with a grim resolution to persevere: "Bear bravely up, my Muse, the way thou went'st before." The contempt for his own age is unmitigated in Drayton's preface "To Any That Will Read It," and emerges with equal vehemence in the railing of the final song against,

> . . . the bestial route, and boorish rabblement
> Of those rude vulgar sots, whose brains are only slime,
> Born to the doting world in this last iron time,
> So stony and so dull, that Orpheus which (men say)
> By the enticing strains of his melodious lay,
> Drew rocks and aged trees to whether he would please,
> He might as well have mov'd the Universe as these. (ll. 6–12)

But, Drayton continues, "leave this fry to Hell in their own filth defiled," and he falls back into his solitary excursion, as if shutting the door forever on the present.

However, if this change in attitude is more than a mere pose, it is also something less than a permanent loss of confidence. The causes for the change lie partly in Drayton's own social outlook at this time (the subject of my next chapter); moreover, a certain amount of disappointment, even bitterness, might have been expected in the last songs of *Poly-Olbion*, for Drayton's *magnum opus*, almost thirty years in the making, had turned out to be his one great publishing failure. He had built a monument to England, and her sons had passed it by. Reading his letter to Drummond and his preface to Part II, I feel that he protests too much—that even he sensed the failure and was willing to let the rest of the stones lie in the quarry. No one can take seriously his promise of "going on with Scotland,"[9] for had he been in earnest he could easily have finished the Scottish songs over the next ten years. Through his friends Alexander and Drummond, he might also have found a publisher in Scotland. The fact that he did not, and that he never again mentions his plan, indicates that in 1622 he simply walked away from the poem. At any rate, Drayton's antiquarian mood seems to have been short-lived; only a few years after the swan song of *Poly-Olbion* he returns to the writing of monumental history.

The Battle of Agincourt

The earlier historical poetry had been preoccupied with the individual roles of heroic men and women in advancing the English nation, but in concentrating on the single personality these poems had fallen short of the truly epic spirit. Essential to epic, as Croce has described it, is the "feeling for human struggles, but for human struggles lit with the light of an aspiration and an ideal, such as one's own people, one's own religious faith and the like, and therefore containing the antitheses of friends and foes, of heroes on both sides, some on the side finally victorious, because protected by God or justice, others upon that which is to be discomfited, subjected, or destroyed."[10] The ideal of *The Battle of Agincourt* (1627) is English nationalism; the hero, distant and impersonal, unlike any of those in Drayton's earlier historical poems: Henry V is a great man placed at the head of his nation, not (like Cromwell or Mortimer) arrogant and aloof from it. Yet, relatively speaking, there is as little characterization of Henry here as there had been in the short "Ballad of Agincourt" twenty years before. Like the "Ballad," this new poem surveys the whole battle, and the greatness of the King is defined by that of his people.

If the diminished focus on personality in the *Battle* sets it apart from Drayton's earlier long poems, the narrative style also shows him advancing along new lines even at this late stage of his life. Surely more than one reader has noticed the unusually panoramic technique with which the English preparations are described. In this graphic depiction of a medieval nation shifting into a war economy the thrill of anticipation seems to grip every citizen. The man "who works for war now thriveth by his trade." Old arms are refurbished; "Tents and pavillions in the fields are pitcht"; cavalry go on field maneuvers; the common soldier "with his pole-axe practiceth the fight"; archers, drummers, and trumpeters sharpen their skills; an old man "with tears of joy" at these sights recalls the field of Crecy and the Black Prince—

> Such were the men of that brave age, quoth he,
> When with his axe he at his foe let drive,
> Morion and scalp down to the teeth could rive. (ll. 326–28)

Village streets are teeming with horses and military traffic; lawyers leave the courts to make wills and testaments; young men leave their ladies. The sun-lit dust clouds raised by troops marching down to embark,

> To the beholder far off standing, shows
> Like some besieged town that were on fire:
> As though foretelling, ere they should return,
> That many a city yet secure must burn. (ll. 251–54)

In this first quarter of the poem, as in the remainder, events are seen through the wide-angle lens: hence the catalogues of ships, families, and shires; the Homeric glimpses of personal courage on the battle-field, like Huntington's and Suffolk's charge for the French banner, or the single combat between Henry and Alençon. Indeed, this is by far the most Homeric of Drayton's poems. Ben Jonson thought so,[11] and such passages as the simile of the French charge at Agincourt bear him out:

> At the full moon look how th' unwieldy tide,
> Shored by some tempest that from sea doth rise
> At the full height, against the ragged side
> Of some rough cliff (of a gigantic size)
> Foaming with rage impetuously doth ride;
> The angry French (in no less furious wise)
> Of men at arms upon their ready horse,
> Assail the English to disperse their force. (ll. 1457–64)

Through it all, the intent is to commemorate the deeds of the nation, so that every character, even Henry, becomes an almost mechanical agent of the national will. Henry's combat with Alençon is purposely located (unhistorically) at the end of the battle, providing a climax to the victory, as if these two heroes epitomized all the strengths and weaknesses of their peoples.

Comparisons between Shakespeare's *Henry V* and *The Battle of Agincourt* are inevitable, and Drayton would have invited them, to judge from the many echoes of the play in his poem. The poem begins, as had the play, with a speech by Chicheley, Archbishop of Canterbury, advising the King on his rights in France. The principal events, preparation for war, Harfleur, and Agincourt, follow in turn. Shakespeare, lacking the paraphernalia that a modern film-maker or theatrical producer would use to produce great battle scenes, provided his audiences with an expansive view of the action through his chorus's prologues. Drayton, writing a poem, was not faced with the same difficulty, but he shows the influence of these prologues as of no other Shakespearean element. In all probability the sweeping overview of Henry's battles was first suggested to him as he listened to the chorus's lines in a performance of this popular play.

The Battle of Agincourt is by no means a verse-adaptation of *Henry V*, however. For one thing, there is little to relieve the severity of Drayton's point of view, particularly in the second half of the poem: no wooing of Katherine, no comic soldiers, no pathetic account of an old comrade babbling of green fields. *Henry V* ends with a full act devoted to Henry's peaceful diplomacy, highlighting the joy incumbent upon his impending marriage. Drayton's poem begins *ab ovo* and ends almost *in medias res*: hard upon the victory at Agincourt comes the King's abrupt departure from the ravaged French countryside. Drayton's restrictive sense of honor did not tolerate cowardice in battle, either, no matter how funny the coward; it is as if Shakespeare's play had been deprived of Bardolph, Pistol, and the low characters, leaving only chivalric pageantry and lofty rhetoric.

These differences between the fullness of life in *Henry V* and the starkness of war in *The Battle of Agincourt* hint at deeper contrasts between Drayton and his fellow countryman. The poetry of Shakespeare is the poetry of inclusion: the King can be at once hero and megalomaniac, the cowardly soldier can find sympathy. Drayton, at least in reacting to the general issue of war and conquest, has none of this negative capability, so that in his poem a colder, more mechanical social and political morality seems to be at work. He sees the slaughter of the French prisoners not as the result of the King's wrath, but as punishment that the French bring on themselves. Only a moment before their executions they were themselves cruelly torturing English prisoners:

> One his bright, sharp-edg'd scimitar doth show,
> Off'ring to lay a thousand crowns (in pride)
> That he two naked English at one blow,
> Bound back to back, will at the waists divide,
> Some bet his sword will do't, some others no,
> After the battle, and they'll have it tried:
> Another wafts his blade about his head,
> And shows them how their hamstrings he will shred.
>   (ll. 1153–60)

They further insult the English King and promise to enslave his nobles. The French abuse of English prisoners of war seems to be entirely Drayton's invention, but it serves to comfort his English readers over the killing of the French prisoners: "After all," Drayton implies, "they would have done as much to us if they'd won."

In spite of all the ringing patriotism, we find in *The Battle of Agincourt* the same elegiac note that sounds through most of Drayton's later poetry—the sense that even man's noblest efforts are tainted. As the poem begins, Drayton is careful to point out the irony of a just war sparked by the selfish ambition of an unjust prelacy. At Harfleur, despite Henry's proclamation for the safety of noncombatants, stray shots cut down nursing mothers, harmless old men, and children. The English soldier, whose bags are stuffed with the wardrobe of French corpses, becomes a swaggering spendthrift,

> And in the tavern in his cups doth roar,
> Chocking his crowns, and grows thereby so bold
> That proudly he a captain's name assumes,
> In his gilt gorget with his tossing plumes. (ll. 2485–88)

The justice of Henry's command notwithstanding, the kind-hearted Englishman who has been told to kill his helpless prisoners, "Turning his face full bitterly doth weep." Yet the ironies of war, like its brilliances, are Homeric, reminding us that Drayton's age, for whom "The gods have destinate / That wretched mortals must live sad,"[12] is in a sense much closer to Homer's than to ours.

The significance of *The Battle of Agincourt* to a contemporary reader lies in England's current difficulties (largely self-induced) with Spain and France. In October 1625 an expedition had gone to Cadiz under Sir Edward Cecil to destroy the Spanish Plate Fleet. After a month's floundering about, the force returned unsuccessful and demoralized. Throughout 1626 England was undergoing military preparations, fearing retaliation from an armada, which Spain was said to be assembling. At the same time, relations with France had heated to the point of open hostilities at sea between ships of the two nations. In the spring of 1627 the Duke of Buckingham undertook his last foolish adventure, the relief of the French Protestants of La Rochelle from siege by the French King. In June 1627 some 84 ships and 10,000 men[13] set sail for the Isle of Rhé, where they arrived only to find that the besieged Protestants did not want their help. Nevertheless, they spent six months trying to take the fortified town of St. Martin, until they were routed by the French army. The survivors of this fiasco returned home in November and spread news of it throughout the land.

This leads me to doubt that *The Battle of Agincourt* was "inspired by the nation's enthusiasm for the cause" of La Rochelle.[14] The impressment of men so soon after the failure at Cadiz, the forced loans extorted by the King and Council from the people, the widespread hatred of its commander, the recently impeached Buckingham, can hardly have made La Rochelle an object of enthusiasm. In fact, Clarendon points out that the war with France (without "so much as the formality of a declaration from the King") "opened the mouths of all men to inveigh against it."[15] If we can rely on Clarendon—a young man at this time—and on the assumption that Drayton reflected here as elsewhere a large segment of public opinion, the likelihood is that the poem was written during the preparations for the Cadiz raid, or in the anxious year following it. Spain, for most Protestant Englishmen, was the real national enemy. Clarendon asserts that the Cadiz action "had been undertaken by the advice of Parliament, and with an universal approbation of the people" and that "The war with Spain had found the nation in a surfeit of a long peace, and in a disposition inclinable enough to war with that nation."[16] Drayton, then, would appear to have been as aroused as other Englishmen at the prospect of a renewed, even hoped-for conflict with Spain. If he approved of the French war, it was only as an extension of his country's long campaign against popery, but he can hardly have met it with the enthusiasm vested in *The Battle of Agincourt.* Moreover, public knowledge of Buckingham's planned expedition would not have been possible until late in the winter of 1626–27, and the poem was registered 16 April 1627, which would allow only a few weeks for the composition of a poem that is both long and well made.

Of the other historical poem published in the 1627 volume, *The Miseries of Queen Margaret,* it must be admitted that the attractions are few. In relating the events of past and present, however, it has much in common with the rest of Drayton's historical poetry. In one sense, Margaret (the villainess of *Henry VI*) is a scourge of God, visited upon the present for the sins of the past; thus the dominant point of view is not Margaret's, but the English people's:

> Yonder she comes when as the people cried,
> Busy with rushes strewing every street;
> The brainless vulgar little understand
> The horrid plagues that ready were to land. (ll. 173–76)

This account of civil war offers an effective contrast to *The Battle of Agincourt*, with its glorious foreign conquests. At the root of the "miseries" that Margaret attends are the usual Elizabethan bugbears: corrupt foreigners, factions, and ambitious nobles. As in *Henry VI*, the rise of Suffolk is closely followed, but here in terms that must surely have put readers in mind of that most hated of their new king's officials, the Duke of Buckingham:

> Hard was the thing that he could not persuade,
> In the King's favor he was so instated
> Without his Suffolk who could not subsist,
> So that he ruled all things as he list. (ll. 117–20)

More interesting, though somewhat conjectural, is the significance of Queen Margaret as the prototype of foreign intruder upon the English throne. She may be intended as a parallel with the newly installed Henrietta Maria—a domestic threat for some by the fact of her much-lamented Catholicism. However, recalling the general outcry against Charles' earlier bid on the Continental marriage market, his Gilbert-and-Sullivan romance in Spain, we are probably safer in identifying her (though only as a type) with the Infanta. This would place the composition some years earlier, when the "Spanish match" was still a live issue, and stylistically the poem does indeed have more in common with the earlier narrative verse than with *The Battle of Agincourt*. The only assurance we have of topicality in this poem is that it appeared at a time when many Englishmen feared that a foreign, Catholic consort would sway the King away from true religion, and would thus bring back to England the civil wars it had known in Queen Margaret's time. So, at least, it must have appeared to Drayton, an aging rural gentleman, who had grown to manhood under an English Protestant Queen, when men believed that the only thing more deleterious to national security than a papist was a foreign papist.

Another narrative poem sandwiched into the 1627 volume probably owes its enduring popularity to its apparent lack of concern with politics, history, or anything else. In the English mock-heroic tradition, *Nymphidia* lies, chronologically and generically, halfway between Chaucer's *Tale of Sir Thopas* and *The Rape of the Lock*: it is partially romance, with its dense umbrage of magic and the supernatural, but it also derives from the Renaissance epic tradition. This means that the poem is no anomaly in Drayton's career, for its subjects are not all that different from those of his serious heroic poetry; only the mood is different. It is a mood that emerges elsewhere with surprising regularity, from the early "Dowsabel" in his *Shepherd's Garland* to the roguish account of divorce proceedings in *The Owl*, the amusingly hyperbolic "Sacrifice to Apollo," not to mention passages in *The Man in the Moon, The Moon-Calf*, and *The Muses' Elysium*. These suggest that for all his seriousness of purpose Drayton had a playful streak, though his humor was not without a moral basis. *Nymphidia* has something to say about mankind, and if the point is made in a comic tone, it does not diminish in importance on that account.

Like *The Barons' Wars* and *Epistles*, this poem is written for an audience, as Drayton says, "In love and arms delighting"; accordingly it reproduces in minature the chief characteristics of Drayton's heroic mode. There are the conventions of Renaissance romance-epic, such as the madness of the hero, the perilous journey, the descent into the underworld, and the climactic single combat between rival lovers; there is even a small heroic epistle from Pigwiggin to Mab. Much of the plot, as others have shown, is influenced by *A Midsummer Night's Dream* and similar accounts of "faery." But the denouement is the author's own, and seen in the light of the rest of the poem, and of Drayton's other poetry, it shows him still turning over familiar ground.

The whole poem hinges on the jealousy of Oberon and the adultery of Pigwiggin, the fierce encounter of the last stanzas growing out of the hatred these two rivals have built up for each other. Drayton's *deus ex machina* is Proserpina, with her cup of Lethe water:

> This Lethe water, you must know,
> The memory destroyeth so,

> That of our weal or of our woe
> Is all remembrance blotted. (ll. 673–76)

No sooner do the two combatants take a sip of this drink than the very grounds for their fighting vanish: King Oberon forgets about Mab's adultery and Pigwiggin forgets about Mab. For men, whose bloodiest quarrels have origins that are usually just as insubstantial as the fairies', the implications are clear: almost all the kinds of problems met with in society—the jealousy, revenge, and human suffering of *The Battle of Agincourt* and *The Miseries of Queen Margaret*—would vanish were it not for our memory of them. In a sense this is Drayton's *Tempest*, where we momentarily abandon our petty hates for the splendid rule of Prospero: "Let us not burden our rememberance with a heaviness that's gone." Yet the realm of Ariel and the "mickle joy and merriment" of the Fairy Court are fantasies, and the hold of the past on men's minds is real and inevitable. With the detached, ironic view of man's pride and prejudice that is typical of his last years, Drayton has taken a momentary excursion into a world where the ancient curse of memory can be dispelled.

In 1629, the late Sir John Beaumont's son published a collection of his father's poetry entitled, after the opening poem, *Bosworth Field*. The attitude of the title poem is in striking contrast with Drayton's historical poetry. Beaumont, thrilled by the clamor of battle and the splendor of Richmond victorious over the hideous Richard III, seems totally insensitive to the innate ugliness of civil war. Furthermore, he goes out of his way to flatter King James and Prince Charles ("God's selected care, and man's delight")—the kind of deference, no doubt, that had helped earn him a baronetcy a few years before. To his friend Drayton, Beaumont's obsequiousness and lack of discernment in so important a matter as English history must have been regrettable. In the otherwise warm eulogy that he published with Beaumont's poetry, Drayton reproaches him for his mundane preoccupations: "Thy care for that which was not worth thy breath / Brought on too soon thy much lamented death." Unlike Beaumont, Drayton was too honest to his idea of poetry, at least in his mature years, to compromise it by flattering the great: a virtue that may account for the high esteem in which so many men of that time held him.[17]

This integrity and straightforwardness, so evident in occasional poems and in the familiar elegies, explains the consistency in devotion to England's past, maintained across three decades, from the *Heroical Epistles* to *The Battle of Agincourt*. Whether these poems are composed around a single person (as are the *Epistles* and *Legends*), or around the panorama of events (as are *Mortimeriados, The Miseries of Queen Margaret,* and *The Battle of Agincourt*), they are always permeated with concern for England's prosperity. From the lessons of the past, in the *Heroical Epistles*, Drayton saw hope for the present; in *Cromwell* and *The Miseries of Queen Margaret* his celebrative tone is replaced by one of admonition and foreboding, which shows through in the grim moments of a poem so ostensibly commemorative as *The Battle of Agincourt*. But in his late years, Drayton seems to have wavered on the point of abandoning hope for the present order, as may appear in the central lines from the poem to Sir John Beaumont:

> My love should build an altar, and thereon
> Should offer up such wreaths as long agone,
> Those daring Grecians, and proud Romans crown'd;
> Giving that honor to their most renown'd.
> But that brave world is past, and we are light,
> After those glorious days, into the night
> Of these base times, which not one Hero have,
> Only an empty title, which the grave
> Shall soon devour; whence it no more shall sound,
> Which never got up higher than the ground.
> Thy care for that which was not worth thy breath
> Brought on too soon thy much lamented death.
> But Heav'n was kind, and would not let thee see
> The plagues that must upon this nation be,
> By whom the Muses have neglected been,
> Which shall add weight and measure to their sin;
> And have already had this curse from us,
> That in their pride they shall grow barbarous.

Past, present, future: Drayton's concern for all England's history is summed up in these three verse paragraphs. We have already seen his vision of the "brave world" of England's past. In order to understand his vision of her future, and to discover the source of his later diffidence about her monumental history, we must place him in the ruins of the Jacobean present.

4 | THE DISORDER OF THE PRESENT

How shall the people hope? how stay their fear,
When old foundations daily are made new?
(Fulke Greville, Lord Brooke, *Alaham*, Chorus of the People)

The Body Politic in *The Owl*

From every indication, Drayton at first hoped for both national and
personal advancement under James I. He published his first tribute
to the King in the final sonnet of the 1600 *Idea*, hailing James as "Of
Kings a Poet and of Poets King." He is more effusive three years
later in a panegyric, "To the Majesty of King James," published in
haste, perhaps even while the Queen was yet unburied. Drayton's
opening lines on his "early Muse" lead us to wonder whether he did
not have the poem in readiness for printing as soon as Elizabeth
died. If so, it would fit into a pathetic, almost comic pattern of bad
luck at gaining patronage—the multiple dedications of the *Heroical
Epistles*, the struggles to hold the eye of the Countess of Bedford,[1]
and the dedication of *Poly-Olbion* to Prince Henry when the young
heir had only a few months to live. The 1603 poem, for its failure
to honor Elizabeth's memory, cancelled out whatever reward Drayton might have deserved, so that he had cause to regret his serene
confidence that he would soon be admitted into the royal circle:

> The praise I give thee shall thy welcome keep
> When all these rude crowds in the dust shall sleep,

77

> And when applause and shouts are hush'd and still,
> Then shall my smooth verse chant thee clear and shrill.

The ensuing slack in Drayton's ardor can be measured in the "Paean Triumphal" to James, composed a year later for the Society of Goldsmiths. Here the King himself receives little direct tribute, the intent being rather to celebrate the visual splendor of a royal progress and the honorable profession of goldsmithery.

These verse-tributes contain little to distinguish Drayton from any of the dozens of poets who scrambled for royal patronage in the first years of James's reign. For evidence that he was seriously concerned about the national government, and alive to the abuses that had crept into the body politic over the previous decade, we must turn to his long satire of 1604, *The Owl*.

This is a transitional poem in two important respects: it is Drayton's first long satire, showing that his range in narrative verse extended beyond the pale of historical poetry; it is also an assessment of things as they stood in the last year of Elizabeth's and the first of James's reign. Although *The Owl* does not show the author's later animosity to the King, the principles that were to spark that animosity are clearly in evidence—the rigid moral code, respect for absolute power, ardent traditionalism. The immense popularity of this poem in the early seventeenth century is owing to its reception as a *roman à clef*, by which news-hungry Englishmen might read gossip about the great, couched in the obscure language that Jonson so effectively ridicules in the banter of Sir Politic Would-Be.

In point of fact, though, Drayton is no Sir Politic; *The Owl* is less a commentary on particular men than a general satire on man, in the medieval tradition of *The Parliament of Birds* and *Mother Hubberd's Tale*. The main question in the reader's mind should have been, not "Who is this?", but "Can this be my society? How are we like birds in this fable?"[2] Admittedly, it is helpful to know that the Vulture in this poem is Secretary Cecil, and it would be nice to know the identity of the Phoenix whom he tries to "taint," but this is only one of the Vulture's many crimes, each of which is categorically recognizable. Again, the Parrot who informs for the Vulture may be modeled on a real spy named Parrat, but this adds nothing to our appreciation of this sedulous bird, of whom we are told only that he

. . . skips
About the private lodging of his Peers:
His eyes were watchful, open were his ears:
He had a tongue for every language fit,
A cheverell conscience, and a searching wit. (ll. 466–70)

In other words, although the uninitiated reader (which class includes all of us) will find a few pieces missing in the puzzle, the full design will be quite clear if the poem is read patiently through.

The whole of *The Owl*—its convention, its temperament, and its very explicit message—is medieval in the sense that it conserves values that had been dying for generations, perhaps over a century. In an earlier chapter we saw Drayton turning from the Marlovian "Renaissance" style of his first two legends to the medievalism of his third, *Robert Duke of Normandy*. The Owl belongs to the same period of reaction. Like *Robert*, it is a dream vision—perhaps the last good poem in that long tradition. The sight of flowers on a May afternoon reminds the dreamer of "Th' inconstant passage of all worldly things"—among which are monarchies "That had their age to win, their hour to lose," and the denizens of monarchies, "wretched souls so ignorantly blind . . . That climb to fall." Like the belling-the-cat episode in *Piers Plowman, The Owl* gives us an entire body politic in an animal world: the Eagle, the great birds of prey (both good and evil), lesser birds of every moral hue, and an owl, who is partly the voice of wisdom, partly that of Drayton himself fulfilling what he believed to be one of the sacred roles of the poet.

The Owl comes to terms with a wide array of contemporary political and social ills—ambition, the neglect of ancient families, usury, rack-renting, marital infidelity, and corruption in churches and courts of law, to name only the principals. Almost every line is a cry against the new directions of the seventeenth century:

The Cormorant set closely to devise
How he might compass strange monopolies.
The gaudy Goldfinch and his courtly mate,
My Madame Bunting, powerful in the State,
Quickly agreed, and but at little stick,
To share a thousand for a Bishopric,

> And scramble us some feathers from the Lark,
> What though a Pastor and a learned clerk? (ll. 377–84)

The panacea for all the problems of society in *The Owl* is to restore the old, clear-cut feudal order, in which the king rules directly, not through his officers: "Let Princes view what their poor subjects try:/ Blind is that sight that's with another's eye" (ll. 589–90). The final admonition of the Eagle is a classic statement of the reciprocal obligations of governor and governed as they were understood in this older form of state:

> Let your wise Fathers an example give,
> And by their rules learn thriftily to live.
> Let those weak birds that want wherewith to fight
> Submit to those that are of grip and might.
> Let those of power the weaker still protect,
> So none shall need his safety to suspect. (ll. 1211–16)

This is rounded out by a passage that is central not only to the poem, but to all of Drayton's thinking about society, if not to most of his contemporaries':

> For when wealth grows into a few men's hands,
> And to the Great, the poor in many bands;
> The pride in Court doth make the Country lean,
> The abject rich hold ancient honor mean.
> Men's wits employ'd to base and servile shifts,
> And laymen taught, by learn'd men's subtle drifts,
> Ill with this State 't must incidentally fare. (ll. 1219–25)

Two important assumptions lie behind this view of the state—the same ones so often implicit in Shakespeare's plays, especially *King Lear*: one is that nature must be the ordering principle in any stable society; the other, that the root of all injustice in the body politic is the violation of this natural order. Just as "th' all seeing Sovereign did disperse Each to his place upon the universe," and thereby maintains control over the rival elements, "So in confusion members are enclos'd, / To frame a State if orderly dispos'd" (ll. 579–80). Orderly disposition is not only required of the monarch, the gentry and the commons; at a time when the City was coming more and more to dominate English culture, men must recognize the needs of the neglected rural people. In the Owl's second sojourn (ll. 747–1058), we leave the Court for the Country, where Drayton expatiates on two much-lamented social evils of his time, the neglect of disabled veterans and the exploiting of the poor by greedy landlords.

The Crane represents those thousands of "aged men at arms" who had served in Elizabeth's army, and who, in spite of national legislation on their behalf, never received compensation for their services.[3] Retiring to the countryside, the Crane tells how he waited in vain for relief from poverty in old age:

> Still fed with words, whilst I with wants did starve
> Having small means, but yet a mighty heart,
> How ere in fame, not honor'd for desert,
> That small I had, I forced was to gage,
> To cure my wounds, and to sustain mine age;
> Whilst those that scarce did ere behold a foe,
> Exult and triumph in my overthrow. (ll. 806–12)

Drayton's scathing portrait of the "cruel Castrel" (kestrel)—the country landlord who abuses his Rooks, or tenants—is an implicit condemnation of modern farming enterprise, as against the medieval customs of communal landholding. This wealthy landlord torments "the poor tenant,"

> Raising new fines, redoubling ancient rent,
> And by th' inclosure of old Common Land
> Racks the dear sweat from his laborious hand,
> Whilst he that digs for breath out of the stones,
> Cracks his stiff sinews, and consumes his bones;
> Yet forc'd to reap continually with strife,
> Snarling contention feeding on his life. (ll. 824–30)

In this disordered world, the landlord, with an eye on a place at Court, sells all the fruits of his tenants' labor for his own profit: "What recks this rank hind if his country starve?" Like the soldier, the old farm laborer too is cast aside without regard for his years of service:

> . . . his claws blunt, and when he can no more,
> The needy Rook is turn'd out of the door:
> And lastly doth his wretchedness bewail,
> A bond-slave to the miserable jail. (ll. 845–48)

The plight of the Crane and the Rook only lends further weight to the Eagle's maxim that "Pride in Court doth make the Country lean."[4]

The City is the third area of erosion in the body politic. There the Pheasant, or prosperous townsman, loses wealth and freedom to the crooked nobility. Our old friend the Court-hungry Castrel, thinking to marry his heir into an affluent family, becomes hopelessly entangled with usurers. At the same time religion, of whatever kind, is almost extinguished: the Catholic Goose, who "humbly doth appeal" goes unheard; the puritan Daw is driven out of church, and the Dove, or true religion, "is left forsaken, and contemn'd of all." This tour through London ends with a visit to the divorce courts, a comic interlude, with an ironic defense of the Cuckoo, on the grounds of the antiquity of his family:

> To him the Ancients temples did erect,
> Which with great pomp and ornament were deckt.
> Th' Italians call him Becco (of a nod)
> With all the reverence that belongs a God. (ll. 983–86)

Nevertheless the verdict goes against the Cuckoo, and his wife is allowed to "have her tail at large."

It is the one light moment in a serious attempt to analyze the corruption in English society and particularly in its administration. Drayton's manifest concern for his country's political welfare had already been apparent in his historical poetry. In *The Owl* these concerns are for the first time embodied in undisguised social criticism: the fear of avaricious and usurping nobility; the contempt for those who, like the Buzzard in ostrich feathers, pretend to honors they do not have; compassion for the neglected people of the countryside. In 1603, however, Drayton did not foresee that the new King to whom he addressed this complaint would soon be compounding these problems.

Drayton and Olcon

At some time during the year or two after publication of *The Owl*, Drayton, and a good many other Englishmen, began to think of King James as more than a little implicated in these abuses of state. Of course royal neglect may have intensified his resentment of the King, but I feel we can place too much weight on suspected personal grievances.[5] As I hope to show in this chapter, Drayton represents a large number of his countrymen in his growing aversion to Elizabeth's successor.

The first traces of ill feeling appear in the *Poems Lyric and Pastoral* of 1606. Here, in the refurbished sixth pastoral of *The Shepherd's Garland*, is the first cryptic reference to a recurring nemesis in Drayton's Jacobean poems, "great Olcon." Drayton's editors have shown this figure to be King James, and I do not think it necessary to review their evidence here.[6] Olcon, says Drayton, "seem'd" a Phoebus to the shepherds at first:

> But he forsakes the herd-grooms and his flocks,
> Nor of his bagpipes takes at all no keep,
> But to the stern wolf and deceitful fox
> Leaves the poor shepherd and his harmless sheep.

A contemporary would have recalled Spenser's moral eclogues here, though I would argue that the passage refers to the Court's inaction when faced with dangerous elements from both left and right. One thing is certain, though: James is disparaged for governmental ineptitude, not for neglecting Drayton. In another eclogue of the same edition Sir Philip Sidney is represented in Heaven, "Laughing even Kings and their delights to scorn," while on earth below, the groves "Are blasted now with the cold northern breath." The "Ode to John Savage" of the 1606 volume proclaims that the only man worth admiring is he,

> Whom the base tyrant's will
> So much could never awe
> As him for good or ill
> From honesty to draw.

This becomes a familiar if necessarily minor strain in later poems, as in the couplet added to the 1619 *Legend of Robert*, "The power of Kings I utterly defy, / Nor am I aw'd by all their tyranny" (ll. 342–43), or in this from the elegy to William Jeffreys, " 'tis alone the monuments of wit, / Above the rage of tyrants that do sit."

The nefarious Olcon returns in *The Shepherd's Sirena*, a poem of unknown date, though certainly composed during James's reign.

It contains one of Drayton's most extraordinary lyric accomplishments, the shepherds' song to Dorilus, and exemplifies the way in which Drayton's strongest external concerns often receive the full measure of his poetic energy. The poem opens with a complaint by the shepherd Dorilus, who has been forced to part from Sirena. In answer to Sirena's plea that he come to her, Dorilus says that he will be killed if he does so. We may suspect, though we can not know for certain, that Dorilus is one of Drayton's patrons, and that his circumstance has political overtones. The meaning of the final third of the poem is unequivocal, however, when "one swain among the rest" (who would seem to be Drayton) calls Dorilus and his friends to action:

> Roguish swineherds that repine
> At our flock, like beastly clowns,
> Swear that they will bring their swine,
> And will root up all our downs. (ll. 356–59)

These are the popular London hacks and ballad writers at whom Drayton so often rails; more generally they signify the encroachment of a whole set of "beastly" values of London and the Court upon rural England. At their head is the greatest hack of the realm:

> Angry Olcon sets them on
> And against us part doth take,
> Ever since he was outgone
> Off'ring rhymes with us to make. (ll. 368–71)

Assuming that this and the earlier Olcon are the same, we must infer that Drayton saw the royal poetaster as envious because he could not cultivate the Muses from his throne; he may have been right. The defiant tone of this passage reminds us that the poetry being defended belongs to a larger tradition of English country life:

> Dearly shall our downs be bought,
> For it never shall be told,
> We our sheep-walks sold for nought. (ll. 373–75)

Direct attacks on the King were unthinkable, so when Drayton could not insult James through recondite allusion, he seems to have resorted to slighting him. This is the tactic behind the closing lines of the "Ballad of Agincourt" ("O, when shall . . . *England* breed again such a King Harry?"), and behind the omission of James from the list of England's rulers in Song XVII of *Poly-Olbion*. For the same reason, the 1600 sonnet to James from *Idea* was trimmed out of the sequence for the great 1619 edition of the *Poems*.

It is hard to believe that this inconspicuous but steady campaign was waged merely out of personal spite, particularly since Drayton's growing hostility toward James parallels the attitude of most knowledgeable Englishmen who did not depend upon the Court for a livelihood. The underlying causes of this general feeling were no doubt inherited from Elizabeth's time, as the whole nation continued the painful transition from feudal to parliamentary government—a movement whose origins lie well before James or any of his Tudor relatives came to the throne. Yet for all his supposed difficulty with Elizabeth, Drayton, like the rest of his generation, has nothing but praise for the Queen (see *Poly-Olbion* XVII.341–52). If he was the sort of person to spite anyone who did not pay him attention, why didn't he treat Elizabeth as he did James? The answer can only lie in the character of the King himself—or in the abuses of his Court, which he both tolerated and actively fostered: the cheapening of titles, the extravagant waste of public funds, his cultivation of worthless favorites or "minions," his refusal to prosecute the war against popery, especially abroad, and his obsequious conduct (as it appeared) toward the Spanish ambassador Count Gondomar.

As a King, James failed on a number of counts, but perhaps on none so grievously as in his failure to understand his subjects' pervasive suspicion of that which was out of the ordinary. Plainness, bluntness, and openness are abiding English values, from Elyot's Pasquil to Shakespeare's Kent, and the great broad-shouldered Englishman could accept neither the waste of the royal treasury nor the King's attempt to compensate for that waste through the selling of titles. At Elizabeth's death there had been about 550 knights in the realm; however, in the first two years of his reign James added more than a thousand to this number. In 1611 the rank of baronet was created, only to be disparaged by commoners as "an honor bought with money"; not surprisingly, within a few years this title, too, was being bartered almost as freely as knighthood.[7] Meanwhile the expenses of the royal household mounted, the Court becoming, in the words of one critic, "a continued masquerado." Observing this scene with a plain Englishman's eye, John Chamberlain wrote in December 1614 that "for all this penurious world, we speak of a masque this Christmas towards which the King gives £1500, the principal motive whereof is thought to be the gracing of young Villiers and to bring him on the stage."[8]

Proclamations of Divine Right notwithstanding, it must have seemed to Chamberlain and other subjects in frequent contact with the Court that England was fast turning into an oligarchy of favorites—especially later in the reign when the enfeebled, nearly senile James turned more and more power over to George Villiers Duke of Buckingham and his cronies. The acrimonious Edward Peyton recalled that the King was "more addicted to love males than females," especially Villiers, whom he "would tumble and kiss as a mistress." Whatever the truth of these rumors—and there was some truth in them—Buckingham's indisputably flamboyant arrogance only exacerbated his countrymen's already-wounded sense of plain decency.[9] Strangely, as if life were imitating art, Buckingham assumed the role of the royal minion, the type whom poets had so often attacked in verse and on the stage. Drayton, writing to Aston's chaplain William Jeffreys in the early 1620s, must have had the Duke in mind when he complained that Virtue's greatest enemies were prospering:

> . . . he that now
> Can do her most disgrace, him they allow
> The time's chief Champion, and he is the man,
> The prize and palm that absolutely won,
> For where the King's closets her free seat hath been,
> She near the lodge not suffered is to inn,
> For ignorance against her stands in state,
> Like some great porter at a palace gate.

The "lodge" alludes unmistakably to the King's favorite pastime of hunting, and if the personification of ignorance is not Buckingham, it certainly epitomizes his type.

Indignation over these perversities at Court was finally brought to a head by a new turn of events in 1620, a critical date in the alienation of the public, Drayton included, from the Court. In August of that year Spain invaded the territory of James's son-in-law Frederick, the Protestant elector of the Palatinate, who was soon driven into exile. After months of vacillating, James called a Parliament to raise money for Frederick, but this body, like its constituents, would not remain silent about the wider implications of the war in Europe.[10] Though James could close the Parliament he could not allay the widespread discontent that it voiced, and he showed his customary stubbornness by refusing to let his Chancellor (Francis Bacon) publish an explanation of the complicated affair for the people. The whole country became fired up over the King's inaction, especially because of the people's already smoldering indignation over the rumored plans for the marriage of Prince Charles to the Infanta. Public discussion of these issues was summarily forbidden. We hear of a man in Stafford arrested for talking in public against Spanish and Jesuit interference in Bohemia; a satirist named Maxwell was put in the Tower for writing on the subject; informers turned in one Francis Poker of Ticknall for criticizing the King, "saying that the Papists would rise again once the Spanish match was completed."[11]

The plight of fellow-Protestants on the Continent aroused memories of England's past exploits abroad, reawakening the spirit of the pike-trailer that slumbered in all true English hearts. In 1624 Drayton's friend John Reynolds admonished the King on the subject of history—earning himself a long stay in jail: "When Scotland was not yet added by your Majesty to England, England (holding herself bound in point of honor) hath sent a black Prince into Spain, a Drake and Essex into Portugal, and an Essex, Willoughby, Norrice, and Fourbisher into France to restore disinherited Kings to their Kingdoms, who were yet but our confederates."[12]

On 17 November 1620, the anniversary of Elizabeth's accession, John Chamberlain commemorated "the happiest day that ever England had," thereby expressing the sentiments of a good part of his generation, who looked back with nostalgia to an earlier time when there were no minions, when the nation was happily at war with the Catholics, and when knighthood and the peerage were honored, conserved, and undiluted. Often the apparent object of this nostalgia was the Queen herself, but even then we can see the thinly disguised idealism, venerating a golden past, viewed hazily and uncritically through the eyes of men living in a crisis that they felt helpless to resolve.[13]

By 1620 Drayton's own hostility to Olcon had increased notice-ably. The year before, in revising *The Owl*, he included an allegor-ical account of the Earl of Somerset and Frances Howard's nefarious romance, in which the reigning Eagle is seen as the dupe.[14] More revealing is the elegy to George Sandys, probably written around the end of 1621—a poem which explains why Drayton published no overt political criticism after 1619, until the King's death:

> I fear as I do stabbing this word State.
> I dare not speak of the Palatinate,
> Although some men make it their hourly theme,
> And talk what's done in Austria and in Beame,
> I may not so; what Spinola intends,
> Nor with his Dutch, which way Prince Maurice bends;
> To other men, although these things be free,
> Yet (George) they must be mysteries to me.

Some have seen in these lines a reference to the royal proclamation of 1620, forbidding public discussion of state affairs. The last coup-let, however, can only mean that Drayton was personally silenced, otherwise there would be no reason to contrast himself with "other men." The lines that follow this couplet also hint at some kind of repressive measures taken against him by those in power: "I scarce dare praise a virtuous friend that's dead, / Lest for my lines he should be censured." In the next part of the elegy, Drayton recalls his "shipwreck" of 1603, owing to his indiscreet haste in saluting James; but this has nothing to do with the source of his more recent troubles. Another elegy of about the same date, written to William Jeffreys, chaplain to Aston during his Spanish embassy, speaks of the 1620 proclamation in more general terms:

> . . . I must write of State, if to Madrid,
> A thing our Proclamations here forbid,
> And that word State such latitude doth bear,
> As it may make me very well to fear
> To write, nay speak at all . . . .

As to the reasons for his personal silencing, Drayton remains mute. A strong likelihood is that he was freer in his vocal than in his writ-ten criticism of the government, and was informed upon by one of the Council's many spies. After all, an associate of known dissidents like Selden and Wither would sooner or later have to be watched.

Men close to Drayton received harsher treatment for voicing their opinions. In his home village of Atherstone, Drayton's uncle Hugh "reviled the King in his drink," according to an informer, for failing to pay his military pension of sixteen pounds. The old man was arrested and flogged, but was saved from further punishment by the testimony of his wife and friends that he was *non compos mentis* from wounds suffered in battle.[15] A few months later, in June 1621, Drayton's friend Wither was examined on charges of printing political satire in *Wither's Motto.* Wither admitted that he "did acquaint diverse of his friends" with the book, "as namely Mr. Drayton, and some other." The investigation of booksellers and suspected buyers continued well into July.[16] At the same time, John Selden was spending a brief time in prison for advising Parliament contrarily to the King's wishes.

These political reprisals undoubtedly had at least two significant effects on Drayton's poetic career at this time. First, they helped bring on the elegiac mood and the crusty antiquarianism of the second part of *Poly-Olbion,* remarked upon in the previous chapter. Drayton's sagging spirits in 1622 remind us that it was a time when popular confidence in the Court had reached its nadir. William Browne, in his melancholy lines affixed to the *Poly-Olbion* of that year, places Drayton's poem in the context of this widespread mood:

> Now, as the people of a famish'd town,
> Receiving no supply, seek up and down
> For moldy corn, and bones long cast aside,
> Wherewith their hunger may be satisfied:
> (Small store now left) we are enforc'd to pry
> And search the dark leaves of Antiquity
> For some good name, to raise our muse again
> In this her crisis.

The restrictions on the press in the early 1620s also explain why many of the poems of *The Battle of Agincourt* volume had to wait until 1627 to be published. The elegies to Sandys and Jeffreys, as we have seen, both contain material in violation of the 1620 proclamation, which Wither had defied. The elegy to William Browne, "Of the evil time," has many characteristics of anti-Jacobean writing, vintage 1620. There is nostalgia for the old order in Drayton's complaint:

> . . . that base villain (not an age yet gone)
> Which a good man would not have look'd upon,
> Now like a God, with divine worship follow'd,
> And all his actions are accounted hollow'd.

And he is equally contemptuous of James's newly minted aristocracy: "Such are by titles lifted to the sky, / As wherefore no man knows, God scarcely why." He objects to the rewarding of spendthrifts who waste their patrimony, while true virtue (as in the elegy to Jeffreys) goes unrewarded. *The Shepherd's Sirena*, whose anti-Jacobean character has already been discussed, was also not published until the 1627 volume. By then, apparently, Drayton no longer felt intimidated: James's proclamations had been safely put to rest with their author; the Duke of Buckingham's influence had waned; the new King was shaping his Spanish policy along lines more amenable to the populace.

One can learn a good deal about Drayton's politics during the Jacobean period by examining his friendships. He seems to have belonged to a rather large circle of men who, if they were not exactly rebels, at least dissented a good part of the time from the policies of the Court. Besides Wither (who had served his first prison term in 1613 for his *Abuses Stript and Whipt*), there was the recalcitrant John Reynolds, one of the most vociferous critics of James's Spanish policy. When Reynolds' sonnet to Drayton appeared on the opening pages of the 1627 *Battle of Agincourt* he had just completed two years in prison for his *Votivae Angliae* and *Vox Coeli*. He had also written commendatory verses for the second part of *Poly-Olbion*. Sir Edward Sackville, fourth Earl of Dorset, to whom Drayton affectionately dedicated his *Muses' Elysium* (1630), was hailed by Reynolds as his "honorable and singular good master." Sackville supported the Virginia Company, to the King's displeasure, and in 1621 James accused him of conspiring with some of the more refractory English lords against the newly elevated Scottish viscounts. George Sandys must have chafed at James's conduct toward the Virginia Company, especially after the imprisonment of his brother Edwin. Both Henry Goodere and Walter Aston, though not overtly critical of James, resented the large debts incurred in the King's service for which they were never compensated. Finally, of course, there was John Selden—hardly a Crown man—whose friendship with Drayton may be traced back at least to 1610.[17]

This is a good time to bring up some questions about Drayton's life, the answers to which might tell us considerably more than we know about the relations between poetry and society in the Jacobean age. First is the matter of Drayton's relations with the circle of Henry Prince of Wales. To many critics of the King's rule, Henry was while he lived the one hope of England's future, for although still in adolescence he showed signs of being unlike his father in every respect. He loved military games, sometimes spending six hours a day in armor. Francis Osborne reports that Henry "in all men's judgments appeared more illustrious than his old father," and it was widely thought that his popularity, combined with his open dislike of James's favorites, made his father uneasy. Drayton had as much reason as anyone to mourn Henry's passing, for his poetry caught the prince's attention, earning him a small annual pension; in the preface of Part II of *Poly-Olbion* he recalls Henry's "princely bounty and usage of me," which encouraged him to persevere in his long poem. He may have come to Henry's attention through the intercession of Sir Walter Aston (one of those "learned and godly men" who according to D'Ewes were the prince's constant companions), but in his patriotism and chivalrousness he is the kind of man the prince would have encouraged. It is unfortunate that more cannot be known about his associations with the circle of Prince Henry.[18]

Another question turns on Drayton's relations with the Inner Temple. The list of his known friends enrolled there (mostly during the first decade of James's reign) includes Selden, Vaughan, Heyward, William Browne, John and Francis Beaumont, Edmund Bolton, William Burton, Christopher Brooke, and John Savage. Another associate, Sir David Murray, was one of several members of Prince Henry's retinue admitted honorarily to the Inner Temple. In 1603, when Walter Aston became a Knight of the Bath, Drayton attended him as esquire and was thereafter entitled to bear arms; the arms are almost exactly the same as those of the Inner Temple, a winged pegasus with a cap of Mercury as crest. During his later years, when in London, Drayton lived in a house on Fleet Street near the Temple. The Inner Temple records do not show that Drayton was ever admitted there, but the facts point to some association with the society. Did the Inner Temple attract a circle of poets and young intellectuals in the early seventeenth century? Or was this coterie part of a larger set of literati from all the Inns? To what extent does Drayton reflect the literary and political views of this group? At present, it seems that any answer to these important questions can only be conjectural.[19]

Hardly conjectural, however, are Drayton's misgivings about the course England had taken since James's accession. In *The Owl*, as in the historical poems before 1603, he had denounced the accelerating changes of the late Elizabethan political order and the men responsible for them. It did not take him long to discover that the new regime would, if anything, only worsen the crisis. He must have felt keenly the Court's neglect of his talents, but it will not do to see this as the source of his resenting the new order. His political criticism (necessarily sometimes vague, general, or even indecipherable) is always a function of his opinion on the whole state of social morality. Again and again in the later poems he reminds us that society has fallen into sin, and that political misrule is a form of punishment ordained for the nation that rejects God's commandments. The effect of this realization on Drayton—as we have seen in the second part of *Poly-Olbion*—is a helpless fatalism: in a depraved society it is fruitless to call for a change in the government, since any government must err in an erring nation. Although such reasoning seems passive and ineffectual, it was arguments of this kind that laid the psychological foundation for the activism of the generation who sat in the Long Parliament, for whom the abuse of authority at Court had become so outrageous that any new form of government was bound to bring improvement.

5 | POETRY AND THE PUBLIC MORALITY

Good farmers in the Country, nurse
The poor that else were undone;
Some landlords spend their money worse
On lust and pride in London.
    There, the roist'rers they play,
    Drab and dice their lands away,
    Which may be ours, another day,
And therefore let's be merry!
        (George Wither, "Christmas Carol," 1622)

"This Ignoble Age"

However artificial it may be as a watershed in English history, the first year of James's reign begins a turning point in Drayton's life. Having found a reliable patron in Sir Walter Aston, he no longer had to work for Henslowe's company. The first poems of this new period, *The Owl* and the 1606 odes, show that his improvement in the craft of poetry was accompanied by a sharper awareness of the poet's role as critic of the present age apart from the past. The "Ode to John Savage" belongs to this group of moral didactic works, as does the ode later entitled "A Skeltoniad." Here we have a poem reminiscent in theme and attitude of several of Jonson's moral lyrics, except that Drayton characteristically incorporates into his ode an element of his native English tradition, the rude Skeltonic:

. . . To retain
The comeliness in mean

> Is true knowledge and wit.
> Not me forc'd rage doth fit,
> That I thereto should lack
> Tobacco, or need sack,
> Which to the colder brain
> Is the true Hippocrene;
> Nor did I ever care
> For great fools, nor them spare.
> Virtue, though neglected,
> Is not so dejected
> As vilely to descend
> To low baseness their end.

His resolution, the poet says, is "How well, and not how much to write"—like the few good men left in the world who care "How well to live, and not how long." In a similar vein the "Defence against the Idle Critic" attacks the values of a "wretched world," which

> With a scornful slightness
> The best things doth disgrace,
> Whilst this strange knowing beast,
> Man, of himself the least,
> His envy declaring,
> Makes Virtue to descend.

These first excursions into satire, along with *The Owl*, exhibit a patient, usually optimistic tone: the body politic may be in a bad way, but it can mend itself if it will only return to the path of nature, which is the path of virtue.

By 1613 Drayton's moral outlook has taken on a darker hue: he writes in Browne's *Britannia's Pastorals* that the sacred groves of poetry are "Now utterly neglected in these days."[1] Beyond the personal disappointment over the reception of *Poly-Olbion*, one senses undertones of the public depression that followed the death of Prince Henry and the Somerset-Howard scandal, with all the portents for England that these events implied. The same year marks the elegy for Penelope Clifton, the virtuous young lady with whom Drayton contrasts the worldly fops crowding the streets of London:

> A thousand silken puppets should have died,

> And in their fulsome coffins putrified,
> Ere in my lines you of their names should hear.

A few years later, he opens one of his finest sonnets with virtually the same image:

> How many paltry, foolish, painted things,
> That now in coaches trouble ev'ry street,
> Shall be forgotten, whom no poet sings,
> Ere they be well wrap'd in their winding sheet?

These lines harbor no mere conceit, but a sincere question, proceeding from an equally sincere contempt for the age, which is to be developed in the elegies of the 1620s. During the five years or so from the writing of these elegies until the publication of *The Battle of Agincourt*, Drayton's spirits were at their lowest. His caustic pessimism is poured out in the three satiric elegies to Browne, Sandys, and Jeffreys, especially in the first, where the condemnation of public morality is unrelenting:

> This isle is a mere bedlam, and therein
> We all lie raving, mad in every sin,
> And him the wisest most men use to call,
> Who doth (alone) the maddest thing of all.

This theme of madness as wisdom reversed is characteristic of the 1627 satires, and is most fully developed in *The Moon-Calf*.

Satiric concerns invade even the pastoral lyrics of 1627, as has already been observed in *The Shepherd's Sirena*. Another of these, *The Quest of Cynthia*, describes a flight from the company of men into a purely natural world, whose wonder and beauty are embodied in the mythic figure of Cynthia. This poem echoes the *Endimion and Phoebe* of thirty years earlier, for in both a female divinity, invested with special powers over nature, attracts the devotion of a male admirer who becomes a recluse from the ordinary world.[2] But here, except for a few verbal parallels, the resemblance ends. Instead of the bookish Platonism and numerology of his apprentice years, Drayton offers the unaffected veneration of woodland nature that is so pervasive in his mature poetry—the world of simples and herbs, "the waxen palace of the bee," "the nimble squirrel," and the trout stream. Formally, this shift in tone is signaled by the use of the simple ballad stanza rather than the weightier pentameter couplets.

The autobiographical implications of this poem begin to intrude when the speaker, to placate Cynthia's anger upon his intrusion, alludes to his past devotion in terms that bespeak the lofty monumentalism of Drayton's earlier work. If I am correct in reading personal reference into these lines (and I do not see how they could be read otherwise), Cynthia is here not only a natural but a national tutelary spirit:

> I first upon the mountains high
> Built altars to thy name;
> And grav'd it on the rocks thereby,
> To propagate thy fame.
>
> I taught the shepherds on the downs,
> Of thee to frame their lays:
> 'Twas I that fill'd the neighboring towns
> With ditties of thy praise. (ll. 153–60)

Not that there should be anything peculiar about the merging of the national with the natural: as a Renaissance Platonic poet, Drayton saw all his earlier work emanating from a real pattern of virtue or excellence: Idea, Phoebe, the spirit of England in *Poly-Olbion*, even Queen Elizabeth in the pastoral song to Beta, are ultimately different manifestations of the same abiding principle of beauty and goodness.

Cynthia is revealed in a bower evocative of Acrasia's famous retreat in *The Faerie Queen* because she stands for a principle antithetical to Spenser's Circean witch. As Acrasia represented the evil in nature-perverted-by-art, Cynthia is the beauty and goodness of nature independent of art. The boughs of trees are her canopy, her jewels are the fireflies, and her perfume the evening dew. Like Acrasia, she has the power to transform the created world, but all her metamorphoses are for man's good. Her offer of refuge is grounded not upon abandonment to sensuality, but upon the contemplation of nature, and it is not without its political overtones:

> The spider's web to watch we'll stand,
> And when it takes the bee,

We'll help, out of the tyrant's hand,
The innocent to free. (ll. 205–8)

Other men, the "idiots" of the "hateful world," fatally attracted by
surfaces, cannot perceive the excellence of this life in nature; their
error is their undoing:

Sometimes we'll angle at the brook,
The freckled trout to take
With silken worms, and bait the hook,
Which him our prey shall make.

Of meddling with such subtle tools,
Such dangers that enclose,
The moral is that painted fools
Are caught with silken shows. (ll. 209–16)

The theme of flight is a familiar one in Drayton's later poetry, yet
the longing to escape is always mitigated by an idealization of the
rustic world unparalleled among other contemporaries.

The contrast between the harmonious world of nature and the
ill-governed city of man is not new to Drayton's poetry. In this regard, *The Quest of Cynthia* is anticipated by the Eagle's speech on
order in *The Owl*, and in *Mortimeriados* by the passage condemning
civil war as especially perverse because it does not appear among the
lower creatures. The doctrine of nature both as standard of conduct
and as object of contemplation in the face of human ugliness is most
succinctly defined in Song XIII of *Poly-Olbion*. The hero of this
song is the hermit who, like the poet in *The Quest of Cynthia*,
chooses to live in the woods apart from men:

This man, that is alone a King in his desire,
By no proud ignorant Lord is basely over-aw'd,
Nor his false praise affects, who grossly being claw'd,
Stands like an itchy moyle; nor of a pin he weighs
What fools, abused Kings, and humorous ladies raise.
His free and noble thought ne'r envies at the grace
That often times is given unto a bawd most base,
Nor stirs it him to think on the impostor vile,
Who seeming what he's not, doth sensually beguile
The sottish purblind world: but absolutely free,
His happy time he spends the works of God to see,

> In those so sundry herbs which there in plenty grow,
> Whose sundry strange effects he only seeks to know. (ll. 184–96)

The rest of this song, indeed the rest of *Poly-Olbion*, amply demonstrates that the study of nature consumed Drayton's energies almost as much as poetry and history, if only because he believed that the happy man is he who knows the workings of nature. This precept need not have come from Lucretius and Virgil; it might well have been learned during his boyhood in the Warwickshire woodlands.

The age's most heinous offense against nature, as Drayton repeatedly complains, is the destruction of England's great forests to make way for the "iron age."[3] He is embittered over the ravaged trees of the Wyre Forest: "Their trunks like aged forks now bare and naked stand, / As for revenge to heaven each held a withered hand." He envisions the ruin of Blackmore Forest by "Man's devouring hand," in a land "Where no man ever plants to our posterity." The Plain of Salisbury prophesies an era "In which all damned sins most vehemently shall rage," when men "scarce shall leave a tree" in seeking to maintain their "luxury and vice." The Forest of Arden, Feckenham Forest, "Great Andredsweld," Warboys Forest, and the rest are victims to a pernicious race of men disdaining both the needs of their posterity and the sanctity of their heritage.

It is chiefly this "unnaturalness" in the age that prompts Drayton's long satire in the 1627 volume, *The Moon-Calf*. Whether this poem, like the elegies, was deliberately withheld from publication until that date is difficult to say, for the political events recalled are few if any. In some respects, it is like *The Owl* in confronting what have been called the most distressing problems of the early seventeenth century: the dislocation of classes, "land fever," which brought on the decline of housekeeping and hospitality in the Country, and extravagant luxury in City and Court.[4] *The Moon-Calf*, however, seems to belong to Drayton's melancholy phase of the early 1620s, for it is permeated with the derisive fatalism of a man who has already made up his mind that his society is on the way to hell.

The first blast of this satire is leveled against the City. The male twin Moon-Calf strikes out for London the moment he can travel:

> . . . where then if he,
> And the familiar butterfly his page,

Can pass the street, the ord'nary, and stage
It is enough; and he himself thinks then
To be the only absolut'st of men. (ll. 284–88)

He falls into all the vices of the City: whoring, gambling, homosexuality, buying Flemish shirts. Finally he sets himself up as what
we should call an intellectual.

The poem touches on a more idiosyncratic London vice in the
1620s, the confusion of masculine and feminine dress. In 1624 the
pious Francis Rous—who ventured into London only to publish his
religious tracts—complained that "This earth that beareth and nour-
isheth us hath been turned into a stage, and women have come forth
acting the parts of men." (A special outrage in that "woman by
creation is inferior to the man.") Henry Fitzgeffrey includes an
epigram in his 1620 collection satirizing "A woman of the masculine
gender." In the same year appeared *Hic Mulier or the Man-woman*,
which reproaches women, especially "the witty offending Great
ones," for wearing "the cloudy, ruffianly broad-brimmed hat and
wanton feather," the immodestly laced French doublet, and short
hair. The swift rebuttal came with *Haec Vir: or the Womanish
Man*, in which the man-woman defends her masculine attire on the
grounds that, since men now dress like women, women are forced
to wear men's clothes if any distinction between the sexes is to be
maintained. Before the year was out, the author of *Hic Mulier* shot
back another pamphlet, *Mul'd Sack*. The controversy was lively but
serious, and many have been related to the growing popular animosity toward the Court, for Francis Osborne later recalled seeing
Buckingham and Somerset often "labor to resemble [ladies] in the
effeminateness of their dressings."[5]

To Drayton, the evil in this fashion lies in its unnatural implications: it signifies the spread of homosexuality and the dominance
of wives over husbands. Once in the city, the male Moon-Calf becomes enamored of a "plump-thigh'd Catamite"; Sodom is "new
risen, and her sin again Embraced by beastly and outrageous men."
In Mother Redcap's fable (ll. 597–828), on the "isle of idiots,"

It went beyond the wit of man to think
The sundry frenzies that he there might see,
One man would to another married be,

> And for a curate taking the town bull
> Would have him tie the knot.[6]

As for the female Moon-Calf, destined to become a mannish "roaring female," any man foolish enough to marry her will "leap Into the burning gulf." The picture of sexual disintegration is more boldly drawn in the vignette describing "a woman, with her buttocks bare, / Got up astride upon a wall-eyed mare, . . ."

> And after her, another that bestrode
> A horse of service; with a lance she rode
> Armed, and behind her on a pillion sat
> Her frantic husband, in a broad brim'd hat,
> A mask and safeguard, and had in his hand
> His mad wife's distaff for a riding wand.[7] (ll. 709–14)

This fantastic caricature of sexual mores presents a travesty of the chivalric knight-errant with his squire and lady; English society had come a long way since its heroic period. Such passages strongly hint that *The Moon-Calf* was directed not only against the City, but also the Court, where (at least by 1620) homosexuality and female dominance were widely rumored to be in vogue.

However, the most recurrent form of social evil satirized in this poem is place-seeking, and the sinister form of pride that drives a man to climb above his appointed rank. It was probably the most consistently harped-on sin in Tudor literature; it is the determining evil in most of Drayton's historical poetry; in *The Moon-Calf* it is the symptom of the age, even the accepted mode of existence: the Moon-Calf is destined to "thrive, when virtuous men do perish." In Mother Bumby's tale (ll. 855–1022), the Witch is glossed as symbolic of

> . . . the ambition men have to be rich
> And great, for which all faith aside they lay,
> And to the Devil give themselves away.

The mule who finds his way into a rich meadow, in Gammer Gurton's tale (ll. 1230–1368), is a parvenu:

> Some crafty fellow that hath slily found
> A way to thrive by; and the fruitful ground
> Is wealth, which he by subtlety doth win,
> In his possession which not long hath been.

A small digression is in order here. Anthony Esler's recent book, *The Aspiring Mind of the Elizabethan Younger Generation*, reminds us that place-seeking was neither new nor shameful in Elizabeth's time. As a younger man Drayton seems to have engaged in this pursuit with the rest of his contemporaries. Like Spenser, he set his sights high, missed, and retired to the less harassing role of spectator-critic. Drayton's friends repeatedly console him on his neglect by the great, and he himself often talks about the same subject.[8] In *The Moon-Calf* he writes,

> Each ignorant sot to honor seeks to rise,
> But as for virtue . . . [she]
> Goes unregarded, that they who should own her
> Dare not take notice ever to have known her. (ll. 243–48)

One is tempted to paraphrase: those who seek honor are not virtuous because virtuous men (like me) are not being rewarded nowadays. There would seem to be a good many sour grapes in Drayton's Jacobean melancholy, although at the risk of being repetitious I should insist that not all of his discontent is owing to personal frustration. By the 1620s the widely known looseness of the Court and its adherents was much deplored, especially in the shires where the strict old Elizabethan moral code was still in force.[9] If anything, Drayton's failure to win favor at Court only secured his course on the road he had first set out upon, in the mainstream of the conservative rural gentry.

Drayton's view of the City in *The Moon-Calf* has already been made apparent, and is consistent with that in *The Owl* (ll. 849 ff.). In the latter poem, the Eagle had warned his birds against lodging in an oak tree that had been set with snares by the fowler. A friend of Drayton's identified this tree as "the city of London," and alongside the Eagle's warning to his subjects he noted, "Had they kept their ancient seats in the country and not basely sojourned at London, they had not been undone by the subtle citizens."[10] The gloss might as well have been Drayton's, for he clearly identified himself with the Thoreauvian hermit in *Poly-Olbion XIII*, who retires "from loathsome airs of smoky cittied towns" to the Warwickshire woodlands. In *Moses* (II.625ff.) Drayton accuses London of infecting England first with her vices, then with the God-sent punishment for them, the 1603 plague. In the first preface to *Poly-Olbion* he heaps scorn on the reader who would prefer "to remain in the thick fogs and mists of ignorance, as near the common lay-stall of a city, refusing to walk forth into Tempe and the fields of the Muses." Similarly in the prelude to Part II of this work he rejects both City and Court:

> Fools gaze at painted courts, to the country let me go,
> To climb the easy hills, then walk the valley low;
> No gold-embossed roofs to me are like the woods;
> No bed like to the grass, nor liquor like the floods:
> A city's but a sink, gay houses gaudy graves,
> The Muses have free leave to starve or live in caves. (XIX.21–26)

Nevertheless, he does not seem to resent the City as such—only as men have made it. His description of London in Song XVI takes due account of the city's panorama and the commercial value of its port; but the song ends with a warning against the "idle gentry" of recent days,

> Now pest'ring all this isle: whose disproportion draws
> The public wealth so dry, and only is the cause
> Our gold goes out so fast, for foolish foreign things,
> Which upstart gentry still into our country brings;
> Who their insatiate pride seek chiefly to maintain
> By that, which only serves to uses vile and vain:
> Which our plain fathers earst would have accounted sin,
> Before the costly coach, and silken stock came in;
> Before that Indian weed so strongly was embrac'd,
> Wherein such mighty sums we prodigally waste;
> That merchants long train'd up in gain's deceitful school,
> And subtly having learn'd to soothe the humorous fool,
> Present their painted toys unto this frantic gull,
> Disparaging our tin, our leather, corn, and wool;
> When foreigners, with ours them warmly clothe and feed,
> Transporting trash to us, of which we ne'er had need. (ll. 343–58)

Thus the evils that are propagated in London and threaten the welfare of all England—pride, avarice, tobacco, usury, extravagance, deference to foreigners—are the same ones that undermine society in *The Owl, The Moon-Calf,* and in most of the historical poems.

Not that there is anything unique in Drayton's loathing the

City. By the early seventeenth century the dominance of London had already made itself felt in the farthest province of England, and resulted in a measure of resentment, if not of envy, among rural people of every class. To these people the evils of the City were virtually indistinct from those of Court life. Drayton likewise condemns both in the same breath, so that here as in most of his satire his bias is absolutely for the Country. In *The Owl* the country Castrel is a rack-renter because he wants to join the Court-set; the logical place for a Moon-Calf to thrive is the City; it is only in the Court and City that sensual aberrations of every kind can flourish unchecked; the trivial business of Court and City distracts the government from the real needs of its least dispensable servants, like the soldier Crane and the country Rook.

Drayton's aversion to the Crown becomes most pronounced, as has been shown, during the early 1620s. It was also at this time that the term "Country" was first becoming current in England to denote the faction, as yet vaguely defined, that opposed the policies of the Crown.[11] Many of Drayton's closest associates during these years had Country allegiances, or if they did not wholly sympathize with the Country, they shared its disdain for the Court. If we understand the political crisis of Jacobean and Caroline England as essentially dependent on this conflict between Court and Country, is it possible to conclude that Drayton belongs in the vanguard of those who eventually turned out the Court in the 1640s?

The question cannot be answered in an absolute way without adopting a simplistic view of the "crisis of confidence" of the early seventeenth century, which Drayton so consistently (and among major poets of his time uniquely, I think) reflects. However, we can single out several important ways in which, by the first decade of the Stuart era, Drayton shows himself in sympathy with many of the younger squirearchy who would later take the side of Parliament. One, the aversion to London, has already been mentioned.[12]

A second point of agreement is in the attitude toward tradition. It has been said of Shakespeare (who at least in his last years was a country gentleman) that his politics and social philosophy reflect the influence of "older forms of thinking,"[13] and at this point it should not be necessary to add that the same applies to Drayton. Tradition is the shaping force in his historical poetry, as it is in the political teaching of *The Owl.* In the early seventeenth century, tradition was the sacred cow and principal legal weapon of Commons, who employed antiquarian scholars to search for precedents that would allow it to thwart the designs of Court and Council. James, in fact, had prevented Camden and others from reviving the Society of Antiquaries in 1614 for fear it would be used for just such purposes.[14]

A moral advantage that Drayton shares with many of the later revolutionists is his independent spirit, somehow maintained in spite of the literary patronage system. In dedicating his *Muses' Elysium,* he boasts to the Earl of Dorset, "I have often adventured upon desperate untrodden ways, which hath drawn some severe censures upon many of my labors, but that neither hath nor can ever trouble me." This kind of "renaissance individualism" may appear at odds with the conservative tenor of so much of his work, but it is in protest against the unconservative, untraditional tendencies that he detected all around him. The same spirit asserts itself repeatedly in the sonnets and other shorter poems as a refusal to follow the current literary fashions.[15] In his more personal poems, like the "Ode to John Savage" or the satiric elegies, it appears as a determination to survive despite the "rage of tyrants" and the baseness of the times. Here again, his sentiments were fundamentally the same as those of the "Country." As one historian has remarked, the dependence of the Court circle on the King "accentuated the psychological gulf between Court and Country, giving the gentry a sense of clear moral superiority over the cringing courtiers."[16]

A final characteristic belief, which is probably an aspect of traditionalism, is in the superiority of the older, more communal way of life as against the competitive and capitalistic. H. R. Trevor-Roper has often maintained that the real social conflict of the early seventeenth century was between the "rising" gentry—place-seeking officials and London merchants—and the "mere" gentry, predominantly rural people who depended on land and rents for a living.[17] If so, in his condemnation of usury, enclosures, and above all place-seeking, Drayton voices the sentiments of most of the second class —the class that was to win at least a temporary victory a generation later. The anti-capitalistic turn of these sentiments is revealed in the outcries against deforestation in *Poly-Olbion,* such as the lament of the Anderida Forest in Song XVII:

What should the builder serve supplies the forger's turn;
When under public good, base private gain takes hold,
And we poor woeful woods, to ruin lastly sold.

These protests are not melancholy pretense; they echo the concerns of thousands of rural people, like the speaker in Commons who deplored the luxury of an age when "women carry manors and thousands of oak trees about their necks."[18] For these men, as for Drayton, private greed—of courtiers, economic adventurers, and even churchmen—was becoming a greater danger to the nation than Spain, popery, or Puritanism.[19]

The Neglect of the Muses

Drayton's comments on the moral and political decline of England under James are almost always joined with complaints on the sad state of poetry and learning: indeed, his social criticism often seems merely a convenient opening for a diatribe against the new poetry and the new ignorance of the seventeenth century. His idea of the poet's office was no less lofty than Milton's, and like Milton he assumed as inevitable the dependence of sound poetry on sound learning. Once again, what emerges from all his views on the state of poetry and learning is the portrait of a man steeped in the traditions of the feudal past and unwilling to see them change.

Repeatedly his Jacobean poetry laments the defiling of the poetic tradition by men of the new "iron age." In a passage added to the eighth eclogue of the 1606 *Pastorals* his shepherds complain that "the rude times their ord'rous matter fling / Into the sacred and once hallowed spring." Some fifteen years later he tells Jeffreys in almost the same language that the sacred springs have been defiled by "a sort of swine." The image of defiling is again used in the prefatory verses to Browne's *Britannia's Pastorals*, when Drayton urges the younger poet to redeem

Those, to the Muses once so sacred, downs,
As no rude foot might there presume to stand
(Now made the way of the unworthiest clowns
Dig'd and plow'd up with each unhallowed hand).

And these lines anticipate those already noted in *The Shepherd's Sirena*, where the shepherds rally to protect their "downs" from Olcon and his swineherds. By this time the aging Drayton seems to have looked back to his Elizabethan days as a golden era, both for himself and for English poetry. In 1619, dedicating the finished version of his *Poems* (almost all of which originate in his Elizabethan period), he explains to Aston that these works "were the fruit of that Muse-nursing season, before this frosty Boreas (I mean the world's coldness) had nipt our flowery Tempe . . . before (I say) Hell had sent up her black Furies that in every corner breathe their venom in the face of clear Poesie." Some months later, Drayton writes to Sandys that nowadays poetry is followed "by groveling drones that never raught her height," so that, like the woman in the Apocalypse, "she must wander in the wilderness."

Among the particular offenders against poetry the foremost were those of the "Momists and satiric sects," like Hall, whom Drayton had once upbraided in some lines to Aston.[20] Momists were a constant bother to Elizabethan and Jacobean poets, however, and Drayton may simply have been following the fashion in denouncing them. On the other hand, he seems to have harbored a special grudge against poets who, instead of publishing their poems, circulated them in manuscript among a private coterie. In the 1613 preface to *Poly-Olbion* he berates the present fashion, "when verses are wholly deduc'd to chambers, and nothing esteem'd in this lunatic age but what is kept in cabinets, and must only pass by transcription." After the roll-call of poets in the elegy to Reynolds, he adds:

> . . . but if you shall
> Say in your knowledge that these be not all
> Have writ in numbers, be inform'd that I
> Only myself to these few men do tie
> Whose works oft printed, set on every post,
> To public censure subject have been most;
> For such whose poems, be they ne'er so rare,
> In private chambers that incloistered are,
> And by transcription daintily must go,
> As though the world unworthy were to know
> Their rich composures, . . .
> I pass not for them. (ll. 181–95)

He is less courteous toward such poets in the outburst in *Poly-Olbion*
XXI. What man deserving to be called a poet, he says,

> . . . envies that their lines in cabinets are kept?
> Though some fantastic fools promote their ragged rhymes,
> And do transcribe them o'er a hundred several times,
> And some fond women win to think them wondrous rare,
> When they lewd beggary trash, nay very gibbrish are. (ll. 180–4)

All the evidence argues that Drayton had in mind here and elsewhere the poetry of Donne and other moderns, like Carew, Henry
King, and Sir Edward Wotton.[21] All four of these poets had verses
circulating in manuscript in the 1610s and 1620s, and they in turn
had courtly imitators by the score whose names we shall probably
never know. What Drayton objected to in this school is clear. First,
its members were probably ambitious young men who had found
favor with the Court. Second, their idea of the poet's office was decidedly un-Spenserian: poetry was no way of life, but simply one
among the many accomplishments of the accomplished gentleman.

The reference to these poets' "ragged rhymes" and "gibbrish"
indicates that there were aesthetic objections behind Drayton's censure. Nourished in the Spenserian school of prosody, Drayton could
not abide verses that, as he says in the same passage of *Poly-Olbion*,
"hobbling run, as with disjointed bones, / And make a viler noise
than carts upon the stones" (ll. 173–74). Then too, he seems to have
resented the obscurity of Donne and other "metaphysicals." Con-
trasting Orpheus with these "mimic apes," he says:

> Had he compos'd his lines like many of these days,
> Which, to be understood, do take it in disdain . . .
> Well might those men have thought the harper had been wood.
>   (ll. 200–4)

In *The Moon-Calf* he warns that true knowledge, and therefore
poetry, is endangered by this false wit:

> Misfortune light on him that aught doth weigh,
> Ye sons of Belial, what ye think or say.
> Who would have thought, whilst wit thought to advance
> Itself so high, damn'd beastly ignorance
> Under the cloak of knowledge should creep in
> And from desert should so much credit win? (ll. 367–72)

No one, it would seem, could be more antithetical to the new tendencies of seventeenth-century poetry than Drayton.[22] In contrast to the apolitical, unhistorical voices of the newer school, Drayton could proclaim as late as the 1627 *Moon-Calf* that the noblest subject of poetry is "Wise policy, morality, or story, / Well portraying the Ancients and their glory" (ll. 407–8). This reaffirms the statement on the function of poetry made in the elegy to Sandys, which complains that nowadays,

> . . . those brave numbers are put by for naught,
> Which rarely read were able to awake
> Bodies from graves, and to the ground to shake
> The wandering clouds, and to our men at arms
> 'Gainst pikes and muskets were most powerful charms. (ll. 80–84)

Conversely, bad poetry is inherently unpatriotic: it lessens England's glory in the eyes of other nations, as is explained in *The Moon-Calf*:

> . . . th' hideous braying of each barbarous ass
> In printed letters freely now must pass,
> In accents so untuneable and vile,
> With other nations as might damn our isle,
> If so our tongue they truly understood,
> And make them think our brains were merely mud. (ll. 391–96)

This contempt for the new fashion and the longing for a return to the older ways of poetry represent another form of contemporary Elizabethan nostalgia, for Drayton was not alone in his dislike of metaphysical poetry. William Drummond's disparagement of "Metaphysical ideas and scholastical quiddities" in poetry is well known. Dudley North also condemned the new vogue of "petty poetry": "The poetry of these times abounds in wit, high conceit, figure, and proportions; thin, light, and empty in matter and substance; like fine colored airy bubbles or quelque-choses, much ostentation and little food." He rejects the new obscurantism as flatly as had Drayton: "These tormentors of their own and their readers' brains I leave to be admired in their high obscure flights. . . . Sophistry and figures may appear fine and witty, but prevail little upon the best judgments." Francis Osborne would have none of this newfangleness, telling his son "to spend no time in reading, much less writing strong lines, which like tough meat ask more pain and time in chewing than can be recompensed by all the nourishment they bring." Drayton's old fireside companion Reynolds, in his censure of modern poetry in *Mythomystes* (c. 1630–32), extolled the works of Chaucer, Sidney, Spenser, Daniel, and Drayton—especially *Poly-Olbion* and *The Battle of Agincourt*—but had only contempt for the novelties of his age.[23]

Drayton's remarks on the decline of poetry, and his specific criticism of the metaphysical school, would seem to place him with a sizeable, somewhat reactionary group of Jacobeans clinging to an older tradition of poetry. We may call it the "Spenserian" tradition, so long as we do not limit it too severely to poets who imitated Spenser.[24] Perhaps a safer label would be the Elizabethan tradition —that which was evoked by Henry Peacham when, in 1620, he addressed an epigram "To Master Michael Drayton":[25]

> What think'st thou, Michael, of our times,
> When only Almanac and ballad rhymes
> Are in request now, where those worthies be
> Who formerly did cherish poesie,
> Where is Augustus? . . .
>
> . . . where's Surrey and
> Our Phoenix Sidney, Essex, Cumberland?
> With numbers more, of whom we are bereft,
> That scarce a prop th' abandoned Muse hath left.

No doubt Peacham expected more than one sympathetic reader.

One of the defining characteristics of this "Elizabethan" group, as may be gathered from Peacham's lines, is its patrician view of literature and the poet—an attitude more typical of feudal than of urban seventeenth-century society. In *The Moon-Calf* Drayton notes the current proliferation of books:

> . . . on the Stationers' stalls, who passing looks,
> To see the multiplicity of books
> That pester it, may well believe the press
> Sick of a surfeit. (ll. 399–402)

Especially harmful are the "lousy pamphlets" on sale everywhere,

> Which now they study, naught but folly learning,
> Which is the cause that they have no discerning

> The good from bad, that well to know,
> Because in ignorance they are nourished so. (ll. 413–16)

Through the tongue-in-cheek *panache* of the "Sacrifice to Apollo" we can discern the same aristocratic spirit. "The profane vulgar are from hence debar'd," he proclaims:

> Let no barbarous groom,
> How brave soe'r he be
> Attempt to enter.

And he urges the dramatists among his "priests of Apollo" to write plays that will rouse their "thick brain'd audience" from its accustomed lethargy.

The poet also has a social eminence that ranks him with the nobility, far above the "profane vulgar." In *The Owl*, he is a "truchman" or interpreter for great men; his function is "To fire their noble hearts with glorious heat." When the Falcon (representing nobility) rescues the Owl from predatory birds, Drayton carefully notes "the natural love of the Falcon to the Owl." Necessary—indeed, divinely ordained—as the patronage system is, however, it puts the poet in danger of selling out.[26] Some, he grants,

> . . . whose minds should be exhal'd and high,
> As free and noble as clear poesie,
> In the slight favor of some lord to come,
> Basely do crouch to his attending groom.
> Immortal gift that art not bought with gold,
> That thou to peasants should be basely sold! (ll. 689–94)

The abuse, however, does not devalue the practice; poets are born to stand behind and a little to the right of kings.

This idea is a logical consequence of the notion, inherited most immediately from Spenser and Sidney, of the divine origin of the poet's role. Here again we find a distinction between the old school and that of Donne, whose concept of the poet is, on the surface at least, far more modest. This sense of the dignity of his role is a notion that Drayton seems to have retained all his life. In the epistle to Geraldine, Drayton's Surrey proclaims that there is "little difference 'twixt the Gods and us," while in *The Owl* poets are called "rare Promethii, fetching fire from Heaven, / To whom the func-

tions of the Gods are given" (ll. 671–72). The shepherd Motto, recalling the origin of the poetic *furor*, tells Rowland in the fifth
eclogue of the *Pastorals* that, "From high Heaven this influence is
breath'd, / The most divine impression of the breast." To the con-
temner of poetry, in *Poly-Olbion* XXI, Drayton responds:

> Slave, he whom thou dost think so mean and poor to be
> Is more than half divine, when he is set by thee. . . .
> He is a God, compar'd with ordinary men. (ll. 137–40)

An emphasis on the person of the poet was to be expected in the
literary theory of those times, given the influence of the Ciceronian
doctrine of *bonus orator bonus vir*. Yet throughout his career Drayton seems to have busied himself about this question almost to the
exclusion of the formal aspects of the poet's craft. His opening lines
in the Reynolds elegy indeed reveal that his earliest fascination was
for the men rather than the work:

> And when that once *Pueriles* I had read,
> And newly had my Cato construed,
> In my small self I greatly marvel'd then,
> Amongst all other, what strange kind of men
> These poets were. (ll. 19–23)

It can justly be argued that had he been less concerned about the
personal dignity of the poet and more attentive to his craft, his reputation might not be what it is today. The more artful but frivolous
poets of the age (as Drayton would have thought of them), like
Carew or Herrick, or the younger Caroline generation, wrote for the
new social classes; thus their compositions, like those of their counterparts on the stage, are as irrelevant to the author's dignity as they
are to the thought and opinion of the time.[27] Not until Milton
would the lofty old marmoreal idea of the poet's talents as "the inspired gift of God rarely bestow'd" be resurrected in England.

The tarnishing of the old standards was, in Drayton's eyes, part
of a more general movement in his society toward ignorance, particularly ignorance of the past. In the 1613 preface to *Poly-Olbion*
he laments the current vogue, "when the idle humorous world must
hear of nothing that either savors of antiquity, or may awake it to
seek after more than dull and slothful ignorance may easily reach

unto." The patriotic implications of this are made evident in the preface to Part II, when he notes, "And some of our outlandish, unnatural English (I know not how otherwise to express them) stick not to say that there is nothing in this island worth studying for, and take a great pride to be ignorant in anything thereof." In the "arsey-varsey" age of perverted values, the man of mode as figured in *The Moon-Calf* is distinguished by his ignorance:

> Knowledge with him is idle, if it strain
> Above the compass of his yeasty brain . . .
> He nothing more than truth and knowledge loathes,
> And nothing he admires of man's but clothes. (ll. 351–58)

Drayton voices the same complaint to Jeffreys:

> So dull and barbarous lately are we grown,
> That for man's knowledge it alone doth make,
> If he can learn to read an Almanac;
> By whom that trash of Amadis of Gaul
> Is held an author most authentical.

He will as soon taste "the great Elixir," he concludes, as live to see "Wit so respected as it was of yore."

Drayton perhaps inherited his respect for learning from a time in his youth when it had not been so available as it was in the relatively sophisticated society of Jacobean England. Moreover, the kind of learning for which he reserved his praise—pre-eminently that supported by the authority of ancient tradition—was fast coming into disrepute among the more enlightened moderns of the seventeenth century. His astronomy is patently Ptolemaic; he believes in barnacle geese; he is attracted to numerology and the occult.

He saw knowledge with the eyes of a medieval scholar—as something to be pursued for its own sake, on a course which would have as little contact as possible with the sordid everyday world. Some such attitude is partly written into his poem on Chapman's translation of Hesoid (1618), which concludes:

> In thy free labors (friend) then rest content.
> Fear not detraction, neither fawn on praise:
> When idle censure all her force hath spent,
> Knowledge can crown herself with her own bays.

The Owl symbolizes in part knowledge above and aloof from the world, as may be gathered from his speech to the Eagle:

> Long have I seen the world's inconstant change,
> Joy moves not me, affliction is not strange.
> I care not for contempt, I seek not fame;
> Knowledge I have and glory in the same. (ll. 337-40)

The true path of knowledge, says Drayton in the same poem (addressing "moral Mantuan"), must lie well away from the beaten highways of the world:

> Who seeks for truth (say'st thou) must tread the path
> Of the sweet private life, which envy's wrath,
> Which poison'd tongues, with vain affected praise,
> Cannot by scorn suppress, by flatt'ry raise. (ll. 651-54)

Nowhere is this view more completely worked out than in Drayton's early *Endimion and Phoebe*, which as we have seen develops the idea that only through knowledge can man attain his highest goal, communion with the one Good, Beautiful, and True. *The Quest of Cynthia* continues this motif, imbued with the wish to escape into a purely natural world. Cynthia's discourse on simples and insects and fairies—in fact all the miscellaneous lore woven into this poem—emerges from a soul long experienced in the solace afforded by rural solitude in the face of the "den of mere despite," which was the world.

In *The Shepherd's Garland* of 1593 Drayton had hailed the late Sir Philip Sidney as the soul of English poetry and learning, as of all else that had been noble in his world then. Sidney, in the fourth eclogue, is the "Spell-charming prophet, sooth-divining seer." In the revised sixth eclogue of 1606, he is the "learned shepherd," "With whose blest spirit (attending him alone) / Virtue to Heaven directly took her flight." In *The Owl*, Sidney is again idealized:

> In him was both the elegance and act.
> O! when that bird was ravish'd from our sight,
> Intombing him the world intomb'd delight. (ll. 1282-84)

What was it about Sidney that so attracted Drayton and others who were discontented over the new directions of poetry, like Drummond and Henry Peacham? It was perhaps the man himself, as he stood enshrined in the writings of his hagiographers: a heroic figure in life and death, adept at poetry, politics, and war, a man of "elegance and act." Amid James's vacillations over the Spanish threat to Protestantism, Sidney's death acquired even greater meaning. He became the chalice of all virtues of the "golden age"—an age that seemed to take on more luster as the moral crisis of the Jacobean age became more acute.

Central to the Sidneian doctrine of poetry was the notion that "the best and most accomplished kind of poetry" was the poetry of action, heroic poetry:

> For as the image of each action stirreth and instructeth the mind, so the lofty image of such worthies most inflameth the mind with desire to be worthy, and informs with counsel how to be worthy. Only let Aeneas be worn in the tablet of your memory, how he governeth himself in the ruin of his country; in the preserving his old father and carrying away his religious ceremonies; . . . how in his inward self, and how in his outward government; and I think, in a mind not prejudiced with a prejudicating humor, he will be found in excellency fruitful.[28]

"Desire to be worthy," "tablet of memory," "outward government" —these are catchwords of a tradition become bankrupt in an age when new classes, having overthrown old standards, had yet to raise their own, so that (to those outsiders who still kept the old ways) worthiness was more often bought than earned, government was determined by expediency, and the tablet of memory crumbled beneath the feet of competitive, ambitious, forward-looking men.

In a copy of the 1619 *Poems* presented to Richard Butcher, Drayton added in manuscript the following lines to his "Ballad of Agincourt":[29]

> When Brownists banish'd be,
> Sects and disloyalty,
> Schism and popery,
> Then shall we flourish;
> And when the great shall aim
> True justice to maintain,
> And shall employ their brain
> Virtue to nourish.

Behind these lines is the same criticism of the body politic as can be found throughout Drayton's Jacobean poetry: no nation can flourish so long as its ruling class—its King, its gentry, its judges, poets, and men of learning—acts from self-interest rather than altruistic motives. The morals of the ruling class will thus determine those of its subjects. A further implication in the very existence of these lines is of course the poet's duty to point out lapses in the government and behavior of a nation. Accordingly, in Drayton's view as in that of the tradition to which he belongs, poetry, ethics, and politics are complementary concerns. In the early seventeenth century, poetry seems to have suffered a special "dissociation of sensibilities" when the old Sidneian poetic yielded to the same intense pressures for change that were rupturing the seams in almost every vessel of culture in England.

6 | ELYSIUM AND AFTER

> *Satyr.* I, seeing the plagues that shortly are to come
> Upon this people, cleanly them forsook,
> And thus am light into Elysium,
> To whose strait search I wholly me betook.
> *Naiis.* Poor silly creature, come along with us, ...
> We to the cheerful presence will thee bring
> Of Jove's dear daughters, where in shades they sit,
> Where thou shalt hear those sacred sisters sing
> Most heavenly hymns, the strength and life of wit.
> *(The Muses' Elysium,* Tenth Nimphall)

The Future of England

As a young man Drayton had seen in his country's history a prophecy of her greatness: England had been purged through civil discord and had purified her church; in war, politics, and poetry she had competed successfully with other nations. But in later years the ruling society that succeeded Elizabeth's seemed to betray that early promise. Little wonder that in both the historical and satiric writing of the 1620s Drayton so often broods on the disparity between past and present. This contrast between the great promise and the grim realization accounts for his ambivalence in forecasting his country's future. On the one hand he maintains hope for a regeneration of the old spirit, if not in England, then at least in the new colonies abroad; yet he is also haunted by the pessimistic reminder, the one common

117

legacy of all history, sacred and profane, that wicked societies bring down upon themselves the wrath of God.

The warning voice prevails in two of the biblical narratives published with *The Muses' Elysium* in 1630, for both *Moses* and *Noah's Flood* are concerned with God's care for a righteous minority while scourging an unjust society; in them Drayton assumes certain parallels between the biblical societies and his own.

The two poems reflect a way of interpreting Scripture that had become common in England during the sixteenth century, especially among Protestants, whereby the reader of the Bible sees his own struggles and the events of his day as reenacting those of biblical times. Medieval men had used biblical stories as *exempla*, of course, or had seen Old Testament characters as "types" of the New, but in the Reformation for the first time since early Christianity we find readers attempting to assess modern in the light of scriptural history —a usage of Scripture that has been called "postfiguration."[1] By this means reformers like John Knox could compare Mary Tudor with Jezebel; John Bale could represent the Pharisees and Sadducees as foreshadowing the medieval monastic orders. Whereas in early church typology the conflict between Jacob and Esau had signified the struggle of early Christians against the pharisaical Jews, in Nicholas Udall's *Jacob and Esau* (1558) the two brothers are the Protestant and the impious Catholic, respectively. The comparison of London with Nineveh in Lodge's *Looking Glass for London and England* (1594) must have seemed obvious to any thoughtful Englishman of that day.

Puritan preachers kept their audience's imagination alive with similar postfigurations of current events. Thomas Gataker's *Anniversary Memorial of England's Delivery from the Spanish Invasion* (1626) is based on a text from Psalm 48, "As with an East wind, thou breakest the ships of Tarshish, so they were destroyed." In the preface to another sermon, *Noah His Obedience* (1623), Gataker points to the evil of his own times and the possibility of a second deluge to punish wicked mankind.[2] Drayton's contemporaries, then, treated the history of the Hebrews much as they did their own history: if the events of Edward II's reign had implications for men living under Elizabeth and James, how much more relevant were the stories of Moses, Joshua, and Samson, since they had been pointed out to men by the Author of all history?

This is not to say that *Moses* and *Noah's Flood* are allegorical reform-pieces on England. They are primarily renditions of sacred history, whose pious motive is to assist the reader of the original text in finding the truths contained therein. This explains the great to-do in *Noah's Flood* about the tonnage of the ark and the extent of the flood—problems with which rationalist scoffers had vexed many of the faithful. The flood, like the plagues in *Moses*, is portrayed as vividly and realistically as possible in order that the reader may see that it all really could have happened exactly as it is described in the Bible.

The application of biblical to contemporary events is thus incidental to the main purpose of these poems, but it is nonetheless important. It seems to have been a familiar practice with Drayton, as when he compares the warning voices of his age with the ancient prophets, in the elegy to Sandys:

> As th'English now, so did the stiff neck'd Jews
> Their noble Prophets utterly refuse,
> And of these men such poor opinions had,
> They counted Esay and Ezechiel mad;
> When Jeremy his Lamentations writ,
> They thought the wizard quite out of his wit,
> Such sots they were, as worthily to lie
> Lock'd in the chains of their captivity.

In *Moses*, a poem first published in 1604, Drayton twice superimposes the modern history of the English on the biblical narrative. After the macabre account of Egypt's plagues in Book II, he addresses "Afflicted London in six hundred three":

> . . . thy affliction serv'd me for a book,
> Whereby to model Egypt's misery,
> When pallid horror did possess thy street. (II.631–33)

The description of the plague, then, is of a piece with the account of London's plagues in Canto IV of *The Barons' Wars*, both serving as a mirror of God's judgments for erring citizens. However, Pharaoh's Egypt is not to be read consistently as representing sinful London. In Book III the overthrow of the army in the Red Sea prompts a comparison with the Armada victory of 1588, "when the Lord with a victorious hand In his high justice scourg'd th' Iberian pride" (ll. 71–72).

Although such overt comparisons are not made in *Noah's Flood*, we know from other sources what the story of Noah meant for Drayton. Mother Red-Cap's Tale, in *The Moon-Calf* (ll. 597–828), is in fact a carefully developed analogue to the Noah legend. On a certain island, the story goes, an old prophecy had it that a deluge would one day come, whose waters would deprive men of their senses. One honest man on the island had often warned the people of this prophecy, "And preach'd to them this deluge (for their good)/ As to th' old world Noe did before the flood." The people ridicule him, however, and he retires to a cave to wait for the end. After a torrential rain he emerges to find that the world has indeed gone mad, and when he tries to win people back to sanity he is driven off and returns to a life of solitude. The moral is pointed at the conclusion: the deluge is "a plague sent by supernatural power Upon the wicked," and

> The rock to which this man for safety climbs
> The contemplation is of the sad times
> Of the declining world . . . .

In the elegy to Browne, the imagery of the flood is again used with contemporary relevance:

> Into the clouds the Devil lately got,
> And by the moisture doubting much the rot,
> A medicine took to make him purge and cast;
> Which in short time began to work so fast,
> That he fell to't, and from his backside flew
> A rout of rascal, a rude ribald crew
> Of base plebeians, which no sooner light
> Upon the earth, but with a sudden flight
> They spread this isle, and as Deucalion once
> Over his shoulder back, by throwing stones
> They became men, even so these beasts became
> Owners of titles from an obscure name.

It is not at all fanciful to suggest that Drayton saw Noah as prefiguring himself and other men of his persuasion in Jacobean

England, particularly since *Noah's Flood* shows a society fallen into those same depravities which he so often finds in his time: men "waxt proud and haughty in their thought." Values were reversed, for "in those times to be just Was to be wicked." The sins of Noah's day, blasphemy, bestiality, incest, even cannibalism, are the results of the same pride and materialism that grip contemporary England, and if the English have not yet sunk to the depths of the antediluvians, it is only because they have not had time enough. The people ridicule Noah as they had laughed at the honest man in *The Moon-Calf*, and perhaps as Drayton felt men were laughing at him, with his quaint, antiquated concerns. Noah's sermon of repentance has about it a ring of current emergency:

> Oh cry for mercy, leave your wicked ways,
> And God from time shall separate those days
> Of vengeance coming, and he shall disperse
> These clouds now threat'ning the whole universe,
> And save the world, which he will else destroy. (ll. 221–25)

Perhaps the claim is insupportable, but the lines of this speech seem charged with the feelings of an old man who saw, as few men could see at that time, the imminent dissolution of his society.

Noah's Flood alternates between these sermons and long passages of natural description, the two of which appear on the surface unrelated. Yet read in the context of Drayton's other poetry, especially *Poly-Olbion* and the *Quest of Cynthia*, these two focal points of the poem offer one of the poet's favorite contrasts—the wonder and variety of Nature as opposed to the monotonous contemptibility of man. Obeying the command of Noah, the animals enter the ark in harmony:

> By the grim wolf the poor sheep safely lay,
> And was his care, which lately was his prey:
> The ass upon the lion leant his head,
> And to the cat the mouse for succor fled. (ll. 305–8)

The people, however, are neither meek nor obedient:

> "Let us but see that God that dares to stand
> To what thou speak'st, . . .
> . . . and we will defy
> Him to his teeth." (ll. 241–45)

The model for man's conduct is the harmonious world of Nature, and all of his perversions may be laid to the revolt against Nature's laws. It is a theme dilated upon in *The Moon-Calf* and implied throughout Drayton's poetry, where the words "sinful" and "unnatural" are practically synonymous.

Both *Moses* and *Noah's Flood*, with the third "divine poem," *David and Goliah*, belong to the line of sacred epic in England, which begins with DuBartas and is consummated in Milton. Some of the poetry in this tradition is purely devotional—either straightforward narrative from Scripture (like *David and Goliah*) or narrative with pious reflection (like Giles Fletcher's *Christ's Victory and Triumph*). The two poems we have been discussing, however, anticipate *Paradise Lost* in their conscious relatedness to contemporary society. Like Milton, Drayton saw the poet as both pastor and judge of society. Nor is Drayton's religious poetry inconsistent with his generally anti-sectarian attitudes, for his overriding intentions of enhancing the truths of Scripture and deterring man from sin are almost one with those of the Christian humanist Milton.

It is significant that in two out of three cases the subject for Drayton's sacred poetry was the regeneration of humanity through its abandonment of an old, sin-laden world for a new land of promise. The final couplet of *Noah's Flood* has the same quiet optimism as the closing lines of *Paradise Lost*: "To make a new world, thus works every one, / The Deluge ceaseth, and the old is gone." In part, this new world is the spiritually renewed world of a society that has undergone expiation for its sins. But another, more specific sense would have occurred to Drayton when he wrote *Moses* and *Noah's Flood*, in which the Promised Land and the new world were both prefigurations of the new land across the Atlantic.

Drayton's great contribution to the mythology of America, the ode "To the Virginian Voyage," has already been discussed in the first chapter of this study; but the imperialism of this poem is not a new note in 1606. In the closing lines of the song to Beta in *The Shepherd's Garland* Drayton had praised Elizabeth as an imperial Queen. The vision of an English empire was also evoked by Mortimer in *England's Heroical Epistles*, Drayton's most prophetic work:

> A thousand kingdoms will we seek from far,
> As many nations waste with civil war;

Where the dishevel'd ghastly sea-nymph sings,
Our well-rig'd ships shall stretch their swelling wings,
And drag their anchors through the sandy foam,
About the world in ev'ry clime to roam,
And those unchrist'ned countries call our own,
Where scarce the name of England hath been known.

In the encomium "To the Majesty of King James," this sense of
empire is the only deeply felt thing. Ironically, the great pacifist and
frustrater of the Virginia colony is told:

Thy Empire bears eight hundred miles in length:
Half which in breadth her bosom forth doth lay
From the fair German to the Vergivian sea:
Thy realm of Ireland, a most fertile land,
Brought in subjection to thy glorious hand,
And all the isles their chalky tops advance
To the sun setting from the coast of France.
Saturn to thee his sovereignty resigns,
Op'ning the lock'd way to the wealthy mines:
And till thy reign Fame all this while did hover,
The Northwest Passage that thou might'st discover
Unto the Indies, where that treasure lies
Whose plenty might ten other worlds suffice.

James's failure to realize these dreams of empire must have only intensified Drayton's ambitions for his country. In the compendium
of English kings in Song XVII of *Poly-Olbion* (from which James
is excluded) he declares of Elizabeth that "scarce any ruled so well"
among all her predecessors. However, the good ruler is not remembered for her un-Jamesian domestic wisdom or her part in establish-
ing true religion. She is said to have ruled well because she

. . . did her power extend
Afflicted France to aid, her own as to defend;
Against th' Iberian rule the Flemings' sure defense:
Rude Ireland's deadly scourge. (ll. 343–46)

Moreover she sent her navy "Unto the either Inde," to Virginia, and
into the very teeth of Spain. In other words her claim to excellence
is identical with that of Henry V, in enhancing the world prestige of
England.

The memorial history of England's seafarers in *Poly-Olbion* XIX—undoubtedly written long before its publication with Part II—is probably the most expansive instance of Drayton's sense of empire. Here the whole sweep of Tudor exploration and adventure is set before us, from Hugh Willoughby's Arctic voyages to Ralegh's ill-fated hunt for gold on the Orinoco. At times Drayton seems almost transported with the romance of geography, as when he tells how Ralph Fitch

> On thence to Ormus set, Goa, Cambaya, then
> To vast Zelabdim, thence to Echubar, again
> Crost Ganges' mighty stream, and his large banks did view,
> To Baccola went on, to Bengola, Pegu;
> And for Mallacan then, Zeiten and Cochin cast,
> Measuring with many a step the great East-Indian waste.
>   (ll. 241–46)

Zanzibar, Bactria, China, Terra Florida, Newfoundland, Puerto Rico, Brazil, Yucatan—the places have captured his imagination as firmly as the men—Drake (the "demi-god at sea"), Frobisher, Cavendish, Hawkins, Gilbert, Barlow, and a score besides, almost all men who won fame in Elizabeth's time.

A commentator on this part of *Poly-Olbion* has found fault with Drayton for misrepresenting the facts as they were given in his un-disputed source, Hakluyt's *Principal Navigations*. Because Drayton's praise for Ralph Lane in Virginia is at odds with the reputation that Hakluyt gave Lane as a bungler, we are told that "Drayton was obviously glozing." On the whole, it is said, Drayton has done "an excellent piece of work in condensing an incalculable number of bare facts into two hundred and fifty lines." However, "when he attempts to tell what each voyager did, he clearly shows a lack of familiarity with his story."[3] Whatever assumptions about poetry this logic may rest on, they are not Drayton's. In the historical poetry he can often be caught misrepresenting a fact in order to embellish a more important truth. The truth of Song XIX is that of England's destiny to world-wide power, realized in the exploits of her greatest heroes, so that he feels at liberty to treat Hakluyt's details with all the nonchalance of a modern historical novelist.

The theme of empire is fairly constant in Drayton's poetry, then, but only in "To the Virginian Voyage" do we find expression of his hopes for a regeneration of the ancient English spirit in the New World. When he wrote his ode, Drayton had no way of knowing as yet how little stomach his King had for imperial exploits; as this became apparent in the ensuing years, the poet's enthusiasm on this point not unexpectedly flagged. In *Poly-Olbion* he seems to consider Virginia as merely one of several opportunities for expanding the empire; he does not single it out as especially important. Later in life, writing to George Sandys in Virginia, Drayton is less than sanguine about America. He asks Sandys for a description of the place, so that he "May become learned in the soil," and inquires about Governor Wyatt's health,

> . . . and how our people there
> Increase and labor . . .
> But you may save your labor if you please,
> To write to me ought of your savages.
> As savage slaves be in Great Britain here,
> As any one that you can show me there.

In a poem of more than a hundred lines, which offered a natural opportunity for expressing his enthusiasm about America, this is not what we should expect from the author of the 1606 ode. Yet Drayton's tone in this elegy is one of concern over the present rather than hope for the future. By the 1620s, although the dream of empire had not vanished, Drayton seems to have realized that England could not bring forth heroes "in regions far" without first renewing the spirit of Agincourt at home.

In fairness to James, we should probably note that his own anti-imperial course followed a path that had been well paved by 1603. Lord Burghley had consistently opposed the adventuring of men like Drake and Ralegh, preferring to stay on good terms with Spain, and to enrich England by commerce with Europe rather than by colonialism and piracy. This policy had been tolerated, if not endorsed by Elizabeth. But from Elizabeth's time on, many subjects found the tide of adventure stronger than the influence of Crown and Council. Drayton's tribute to Elizabeth as a builder of empire, then, is properly seen as one more of those myths conjured up in the Elizabethan nostalgia of the 1610s and 1620s. The old Queen, Ralegh, and the Virginia voyagers had all been fused into a single romantic artifice, made to seem all the more life-like by James's refusal to compete with Spain abroad. By 1622 the author of *Tom Tell-Troath* could feel sure of his historical grounds when telling James that because of his failure to colonize and exploit the East Indies and America, "we have lived to see the brave stock of sovereign reputation, which our great queen your predecessor left us, quite banished and brought to nothing."[4]

Many of Drayton's associates seem to have been equally attracted to the possibilities of colonization, especially in America. Robert Hayman sent Drayton a friendly epigram in his *Quodlibets* (1628), which had, as the title page says, "lately come over from New Britaniola." George Wither wrote some eulogistic verses for Hayman, also a poem for John Smith's *Description of New England,* which bears resemblances to Drayton's "Virginian Voyage." In New England, Wither writes, men will be able "to repair what time and pride decays In this rich kingdom":

> The proud Iberians shall not rule those seas,
> To check our ships from sailing where they please;
> Nor future time make any foreign power
> Become so great to force a bound to our.

A more prominent friend, Sir William Alexander, attempted to colonize Nova Scotia in 1621, only to meet with frustration from the very King who had granted him the land. Without question, whether Drayton's friends were active entrepreneurs like Alexander, Sandys, and Hayman, or merely avid supporters like Wither, they must have stimulated his hopes for a future overseas English empire.

The future of England is of course a central concern in many poems besides those discussed in this chapter. Drayton was too much the political visionary in his historical poetry not to provide England with adumbrations of her future glory (as in the *Heroical Epistles*) or her imminent retribution (as in *The Barons' Wars*). In the satires he adopts the voice of the reformer, warning his countrymen of the consequences of their folly. Even the short "Ballad of Agincourt" ends on a note of concern for the future. Drayton's poems of empire ("To the Majesty of King James," "To the Virginian Voyage," and Song XIX of *Poly-Olbion*), then, ought not to be thought of as occasional pieces, given the context of the rest of his work. Admittedly, these "poems of empire" are scarcely numerous enough to deserve a label, but they add an important dimension to Drayton's stature as a public poet. In the later heyday of the British Empire a whole mob of jingoist laureates would alternate between romanticizing the English past and entertaining visions of her future. If this puts Drayton in undistinguished company, it may at least be said of him that he was honest and that he was first.

The impress of the public poet is also on the divine poems of 1630, which are written from a fully integrated sense of the poet's religious, moral, and political office in society. When we find, looking back over forty years, that his last published poems were taken from the same source as his first, we realize the deep religious commitment that lay behind even his most worldly poetry. Whatever a reader might think of this quality, it must account in no small way for that perdurable serenity that is Drayton's greatest charm, even in some of his least successful efforts.

The Muses' Elysium

The last poems of 1630 mark a return to Drayton's earliest forms in yet another sense, for *The Muses' Elysium*, different though it is from everything that had been written in the pastoral tradition, at least has its roots in the conventional eclogues of *The Shepherd's Garland*. However, these ten nimphalls, as Drayton calls them, are not mere valedictory pieces. If, as Frank Kermode has said, "The first consideration of pastoral poetry is that there should be a sharp difference between two ways of life, the rustic and the urban,"[5] then a return to pastoralism at this stage of Drayton's life is precisely what we should have expected. I would even go so far as to say that the freshness and beauty of the best poems in *The Muses' Elysium* derive mainly from the sharpness of the author's aversion to life in the Court and City.

This underlying mood is not quickly to be discovered by anyone looking at the nimphalls in isolation from the rest of Drayton's work. Reading the airy "Description of Elysium" and the frivolous opening nimphall, one is likely to agree with C. S. Lewis on the whole sequence: "Nothing more Golden had ever been produced. They teach nothing, assert nothing, depict almost nothing; or if anything, Scaliger's and Sidney's *naturam alteram*."[6] A good part of *The Muses' Elysium* is given to the old bachelor's ruminations about suffering in love, which do indeed teach us nothing, charming though they may be. Yet there is something more.

The Fourth Nimphall describes a journey outside Elysium to "Felicia's fields," a land that is both alien and fearful to the nymph Cloris:

> But there such monstrous shapes I saw,
> That to this hour affright me.
> Through the thick hair that thatch'd their brows
> Their eyes upon me stared,
> Like to those raging, frantic frows
> For Bacchus' feasts prepared:
> Their bodies, although straight by kind,
> Yet they so monstrous make them,
> That for huge bags blown up with wind,
> You very well may take them.
> Their bowels in their elbows are,
> Whereon depend their paunches,
> And their deformed arms by far
> Made larger than their haunches.

Felicia is, of course, a foil to Elysium, and the wretchedness of the Felicians is a minor theme in the remaining nimphalls. At the end of the Fifth Nimphall the old hermit Clarinax, who knows the powers of herbs and reveres Antiquity, is called away "To cure a madman, which of late / Is from Felicia sent me." In one of the best, the Seventh Nimphall, Venus ("The fond Felicians are her common game") enters Felicia disguised as an old fortune teller, with Cupid as her "zany," handling her luggage. As the Elysian spies tell it, Venus' sales pitch is no less successful with the Felicians than is her disguise:

> "Come, my fair girls, let's see, what will you buy?
> Here be fine night masks, plastered well within,
> To supple wrinkles and to smooth the skin:
> Here's crystal, coral, bugle, jet in beads,
> Cornelian bracelets for my dainty maids."

> Then periwigs and sear-cloth gloves doth show,
> To make their hands as white as swan or snow:
> Then takes she forth a curious gilded box,
> Which was not opened but by double locks;
> Takes them aside and doth a paper spread,
> In which was painting both for white and red:
> And next a piece of silk, wherein there lies,
> For the decay'd, false breasts, false teeth, false eyes.

Where or what, we may ask, is Felicia? It is a fair question, given the customary topicality of English Renaissance pastoral. According to Drayton's editors, Felicia is an "ironic name for the real world." I believe that a more precise identification can be made with contemporary England. The "madness" of the Felicians, their outlandish fashions, the "fondness" of their sexual morality—all remind us of the follies of Englishmen as they are satirized in *The Moon-Calf* and the elegies. What is more, "felicia" is a Latin equivalent for the Greek word that gave the title of *Poly-Olbion*.

The strongest evidence for interpreting Felicia as England comes in the last nimphall, in which the Elysians give shelter to an old satyr, a fugitive who complains that

> . . . fair Felicia which was but of late
> Earth's paradise, that never had her peer,
> Stands now in that most lamentable state
> That not a Sylvan will inhabit there.

The satyr is Drayton himself (the pastoral poet traditionally represents himself in his eclogues), and his indictment of the destroyers of England is the culmination of his long campaign against the "beastly men" (as he called them in *Poly-Olbion*) who were laying waste his country's forests and fields:

> The lofty high wood and the lower spring,
> Shelt'ring the deer, in many a sudden shower,
> Where choirs of birds oft wonted were to sing,
> The flaming furnace wholly doth devour.

And the satyr looks forward, as did Drayton, to "those plagues their next posterity shall see"—the punishment for the Felicians' abuse of nature. In what amounts to a formal summing-up of the main concerns of his mature life, Drayton has his satyr explain what finally drove him from the Felicians. Foremost was their contempt for the past:

> This beastly brood by no means may abide
> The name of their brave ancestors to hear,
> By whom their sordid slavery is descried
> So unlike them as though not theirs they were.

Second, they have neglected their poetic heritage:

> Nor yet they sense, nor understanding have
> Of those brave Muses that their country sang,
> But with false lips ignobly do deprave
> The right and honor that to them belong.

Last, he reaffirms their crimes against Nature:

> This cruel kind thus viper-like devour
> That fruitful soil which them too fully fed;
> The earth doth curse the age, and every hour
> Again, that it these vip'rous monsters bred.

A pointless aside, perhaps, but one wonders what Drayton would have said had he been around in 1941, when Felicia's descendants, in order to make way for a road, tore down the house that was traditionally marked as his birthplace.

In any event it will not do to see *The Muses' Elysium* as entirely "Golden." The Golden poetry of the Elizabethans lies behind these poems, of course, especially in the seventh Nimphall, where the ferryman's monologue is modeled on the poem in Greene's *Francesco's Fortunes* (1590) called "Eurymachus' Fancy." Greene's poem does partake of the airy lightness that Lewis associates with Golden poetry; indeed, the poem is little more than an extended Petrarchan complaint done up in the novel guise of a ferryman's song. As in Greene's poem, Venus and Cupid hail an unsuspecting ferryman whose failure to recognize the pair is the source of the amusing irony at the heart of the poem. But Drayton's ferryman Codrus is a gruff old yeoman whose forthrightness and simplicity will not allow for the subtle paradoxes of fancy passion. Codrus finds that the blind boy's hands are too soft for any worthwhile trade, and refuses to believe in his skill at archery. This rusticity neatly offsets Venus' sly urbanity as well as the high romance of most of the Elysian scenes. Venus has the last word, but as Codrus tells the Nymphs, he remains unconvinced; thus, he is rather like the low comic characters of an Elizabethan dramatic subplot, reminding us of another dimension of human life beyond this pastoral enclave. In general, I believe it can be said that thought and feeling are more complex in this poem than in most of the Golden lyrics of Greene and his contemporaries.

Like much great pastoral poetry, *The Muses' Elysium* is both topical and Arcadian, sharing a common ground with satire in the longing for a return to the simple life of an earlier generation, while scorning the vices of urban, mercantile society.[7] Nor will it do to see Drayton as the escapist-idealist in flight from the real world. True, in much of Drayton's later poetry we find a longing for escape, like that of the Hermit in *Poly-Olbion* who,

> . . . with a constant mind
> Man's beastliness so loathes, that flying human kind,
> The black and darksome nights, the bright and gladsome days
> Indifferent are to him, his hope on God that stays. (XIII.177–80)

But escapism implies a measure of self-deceit, and Drayton never deceives himself about the nature of England's sickness and the terrible consequences it must entail. In the face of disillusionment, he remains conscious of the whole of experience, for the bitterness of the last is offset by the naïve fancies of the earlier nimphalls, which are indeed "pure Golden."

If Felicia is England, what, finally, can be made of Elysium? Kathleen Tillotson has rightly emphasized that "It is the *Muses'* Elysium, the *Poets'* paradise, with Apollo as its tutelary deity," and that it also signifies "a hint of Elizabeth's reign, that long-ago golden age for poets."[8] Its precise meaning is as impossibly elusive as any intensely personal symbol, but it also seems to imply simple rusticity, where men live in harmony with Nature and women are no more deceitful than they need to be. Such a haven Drayton, the old fugitive satyr, may really have found with the Earl of Dorset, as others have suggested. But it is just as likely that the rural Elysium of his boyhood in Warwickshire also lies among the associations behind this symbol.

Drayton spent the last summer of his life at the Gloucester home of his boyhood master's daughter Anne, where he wrote a final letter to Drummond. Shortly after Drayton's death, Drummond eulogized him in a letter to their mutual friend, Sir William Alexander: "Of all the good race of poets who wrote in the time of Queen Elizabeth," he said, "your Lordship now alone remains."[9]

Perhaps some such feelings were behind the decision to bury Drayton in Westminster Abbey. It was not so much the poetry that Drummond and a good many others venerated (although it was worth venerating), but the man—in the time of Charles I, a living relic among young poets and writers who had never seen Sidney or Spenser or Marlowe, a memento of a period in English civilization fast becoming legendary. Already in 1622 William Browne recognized Drayton as the last Elizabethan:

> Immortal Sidney, honored Colin Clout,
> Presaging what we feel, went timely out.
> Then why lives Drayton, when the times refuse
> Both means to live, and matter for a Muse?
> Only without excuse to leave us quite,
> And tell us, Durst we act, he durst to write.

George Wither, too, if it was he who wrote "The Great Assizes Holden in Parnassus" (1645), recognized Drayton's place in the old tradition, defending him against charges of homeliness by the subtle, smoother wits of a later generation.[10]

For all his antiquated ways—and from the standpoint of fashion they had a faint mustiness almost from the beginning—Drayton's sentiments place him among the increasingly vocal faction of his day known as "the Country," which one historian has aptly described as "that large, indeterminate, unpolitical, but highly sensitive miscellany of men," who would rebel "not against the monarchy (they had long clung to monarchist beliefs) nor against economic archaism (it was they who were the archaists), but against the vast, oppressive, ever-extending apparatus of parasitic bureaucracy which had grown up around the throne and above the economy of England."[11] Drayton is one of the few articulate literary spokesmen for the Country at a time when virtually all the worthwhile English poetry belongs to the ambience of Court and City. Poets of this milieu, with its sophisticated liberality and ease, are seldom moved to protest against laxity in government or against desecration of nature and tradition.

Drayton's poetry must have had a large audience, given the frequency with which his works were reprinted in the earlier seventeenth century, but what kind of readers were they? I have given some account of the friends and associates who form the core of this audience, many of whom, like Drayton, had roots in the English midlands, with its viable tradition of non-conformism and independence.[12] They do not seem to have shared the tastes, let alone the values, of those who enjoyed Donne, Carew, Herrick, or the Cavaliers. Nor was Drayton's readership like that of Ben Jonson, which consisted of "small circles in which aristocratic and cultivated people knew each other intimately."[13] On the contrary, it is fairly certain that Drayton was attempting to write for a national audience, as is hinted in his dedicating the 1627 volume to "the noblest gentlemen of these renowned Kingdoms of Great Britain." This widespread, but civilized, educated public, like as not unaware of current literary fashions in London, still preferred to read the older "medieval" kinds of poetry so dear to the yeoman Harpool in *Sir John Oldcastle*: "English books . . . that I'll not part with for your bishopric: Bevis of Hampton, Owleglass, the Friar and the Boy, Ellen of Rumming, Robin Hood, and other such goodly stories." The catalogue is reminiscent of the famous library of Captain Cox of Coventry, with its generous selection of Skelton, tales about Huon of Bordeaux, Bevis, and Robin Hood, not to mention the popular ballads.[14] By the 1620s most urbane Englishmen would have dismissed the taste for such works as crude and old-fashioned, though it coincides well with the rough, active vitality of poems like the "Ballad of Agincourt." The fact of a large, widely dispersed audience of course requires that a poet's work be printed, while that for a coterie does not, and this may explain in part Drayton's insistence on publication, in contrast with Donne, Herbert, or Jonson.

We know all too little about literary taste and fashion outside the Court and City in seventeenth-century England, and it may be that this ignorance has contributed to the neglect of Drayton by cultural historians of the period. He simply does not fit into the picture of the age as we have received it from Grierson, Eliot, Willey, and others.[15] It is a century of doubt, intellectual searching, and revolt; Drayton is a poet of traditions, affirmations, and allegiances—a patriot when the role was out of fashion. Or was it? Any view of any age is to some extent a fiction, but a view of the seventeenth century that excludes the opinions and aspirations of that sizeable class of Englishmen to which Drayton belonged is more fictitious than it need be. Perhaps if we knew more about the literary tastes of this class as well as other segments of the population, we could retool our shopworn, inadequate methods of classifying seventeenth-century poets (the School of Spenser, the Metaphysicals, the Tribe of Ben—a taxonomy that can neither be used nor defended). Such knowledge might also undo much that needs to be un-Donne, expanding our views of English culture and its directions in the seventeenth century.

It can be argued, for instance, that with all his medievalness (his poems in the dream-vision and *de casibus* traditions, his satire on the estates, his desire to keep alive a defunct feudal political philosophy, his distaste for the "modern") Drayton anticipates much that is to come in the later seventeenth century. As Lawrence Stone has written, "it is . . . between 1560 and 1640, and more precisely between 1580 and 1620, that the real watershed between medieval and modern England must be placed."[16] No poet better substantiates this thesis than Drayton, both in his own chronology and in his Janus-like role among contemporaries. I have already described the premonitions of the Civil War in his work, but beyond that there is the poetry itself—the heroic couplets, the penchant for natural description—often sounding more Neo-Classical than Elizabethan. The *Heroical Epistles, Poly-Olbion*, and the divine poems are for the most part essays in the poetry of statement, and perhaps because of this tendency in its own poetry, the eighteenth century seems to have found Drayton's work rather more to its liking than, say, Donne's or Crashaw's. A fairly authoritative voice of that age remarked, while discussing the influence of Drayton's heroic couplets, "It is easy for those who are conversant with our author's works to see how much the moderns and even Mr. Pope himself copy Mr. Drayton, and refine upon him in those distinctions which are esteemed the most delicate improvements of our English versification, such as the turns, the pauses, the elegant tautologies, &c."[17]

Drayton also shares the Neo-Classical sense of the public man, a concern so dominant in his poetry that characters and lyric personae are often intolerably flat and two dimensional.[18] This is explained in that, taken as a whole, his poetry chronicles the moment in English history when the society became aware of itself as a nation. Drayton carries on the epideicticism of medieval and Renaissaance poetry, with origins that reach into remote human antiquity,[19] but there is a difference; for whereas the earlier poets grounded their praise and blame in the deeds of single men or factions, Drayton's subject is finally his whole nation. The Britannia on the title page of *Poly-Olbion* is a mythic depiction of the national self, as venerable as Arthur, Alexander, or any of the old "worthies." Drayton's work thus belongs to an era in the history of European poetry that begins with Camoens and Tasso and continues through Tolstoy. This transition from individual to national epideicticism corresponds to the change that takes place in the chivalric hero. On the surface, the world of Drayton's narratives resembles that of Malory's romances —a world of courtly amours, tournaments, single combats, and the like; but the fortunes of Mortimer, Robert of Normandy, the Black Prince, and others in Drayton's pantheon are inextricably grafted to those of the whole nation. In *The Battle of Agincourt* the old quest for fame and personal virtue becomes a search for national fulfillment, just as, in Tudor society, the old chivalric knight yielded precedence to the statesman and field general.[20] Drayton's heroes belong ostensibly to the chivalric tradition, but they derive their real significance from their roles in government—or, as in the cases of Gaveston or Queen Margaret, in the undoing of government.

Men and events also lose their contours to an idealistic concept of history, monumental history, not unlike that which certain educators would have us return to American schoolrooms—"the wonderful tales from American history," such as the first Thanksgiving or the legends about Washington, rather than the ugly facts of slavery and abuse of the Indians.[21] It is the kind of instruction Drayton would have endorsed, for notwithstanding his own demands for learning and accuracy, he was not above coloring the facts; Truth was more important than the facts. Accordingly (as was noted in Chapter 2) he could change a place-name in order to accommodate his story to the Arthurian legend. He rivals Hakluyt in glorifying the English voyagers, and if he misrepresents an episode from the *Principal Navigations* it is only because the Truth of English excellence is thereby more apparent. This tendency, I believe, explains

Drayton's preference for the authority of tradition over what we should call solid historical evidence, most prominently argued in Song X of *Poly-Olbion*. Perhaps it is also the kind of idealism that inspires a sixty-eight-year-old man to write a love poem the night before he dies.

The substance of Drayton's idealism, including the vision of a great nation extending its noble presence all over the globe, may have little to recommend itself to the last generation of the twentieth century. A great deal must be said, however, for his consistency of purpose. Aubrey reports that at Selden's funeral the minister said, "If learning could have kept a man alive, our brother had not died." Something similar might have been said of Drayton, not just with respect to his learning, but especially regarding his devotion to England and English poetry. The unfaltering adherence to these causes over half a century of literary activity affirms Drayton's role as a poet of fixed, permanent things, a near-perfect type of the conservative mind. Not for nothing is *Poly-Olbion* rooted in the land of England, the thing that changes least as its generations of men pass away. Had he lived at a more stable time in English history—say a century later—he might never have accomplished as much as he did, for the very transitoriness of morality, politics, and poetry in the early seventeenth century only heightened the eloquence with which he sought to enlighten an erring society in the ways of nature and the past.

Appendix A
Four Odes by Drayton

To the Virginian Voyage

You brave heroic minds,
Worthy your country's name,
That honor still pursue,
Go, and subdue,
Whilst loit'ring hinds
Lurk here at home, with shame.

Britans, you stay too long,
Quickly aboard bestow you,
And with a merry gale
Swell your stretch'd sail,
With vows as strong
As the winds that blow you.

Your course securely steer,
West and by South forth keep.
Rocks, lee-shores, nor shoals,
When Eolus scowls,
You need not fear,
So absolute the deep.

And cheerfully at sea,
Success you still entice
To get the pearl and gold,
And ours to hold,
VIRGINIA
Earth's only Paradise.

Where Nature hath in store
Fowl, venison, and fish,
And the fruitfull'st soil,
Without your toil,
Three harvests more,
All greater than your wish.

And the ambitious vine
Crowns with his purple mass,
The cedar reaching high
To kiss the sky,
The cypress, pine
And useful sassafras.

To whose, the golden age
Still Nature's laws doth give,
Nor other cares that tend,
But them to defend
From Winter's age,
That long there doth not live.

When as the luscious smell
Of that delicious land,
Above the seas that flows
The clear wind throws,
Your hearts to swell
Approaching the dear strand,

In kenning of the shore
(Thanks to God first given)
O you the happy'st men,
Be frolic then,
Let cannons roar,
Frighting the wide Heaven.

And in regions far
Such Heroes bring ye forth,
As those from whom we came,
And plant our name
Under that star
Not known unto our North.

And as there plenty grows
Of laurel everywhere,
Apollo's sacred tree,
You it may see
A poet's brows
To crown, that may sing there.

Thy voyage attend,
Industrious Hakluyt,
Whose reading shall inflame
Men to seek fame,
And much commend
To after-times thy wit.

An Ode Written in the Peak

This while we are abroad,
Shall we not touch our lyre?
Shall we not sing an ode?
Shall that holy fire,
In us that strongly glowed,
In this cold air expire?

Long since the Summer laid
Her lusty brav'ry down,
The autumn half is weigh'd,
And Boreas 'gins to frown,
Since now I did behold
Great Brut's first-builded town.

Though in the utmost Peak
A while we do remain,
Amongst the mountains bleak
Expos'd to sleet and rain,
No sport our hours shall break,
To exercise our vein.

What though bright Phoebus' beams
Refresh the southern ground,
And though the princely Thames

With beauteous nymphs abound,
And by old Camber's streams
Be many wonders found;

Yet many rivers clear
Here glide in silver swathes,
And what of all most dear,
Buxton's delicious baths,
Strong ale and noble cheer,
T' assuage breme Winter's scathes.

Those grim and horrid caves,
Whose looks affright the day,
Wherein nice Nature saves
What she would not bewray,
Our better leisure craves,
And doth invite our lay.

In places far or near,
Or famous, or obscure,
Where wholesome is the air,
Or where the most impure,
All times, and everywhere,
The Muse is still in ure.

A Hymn to His Lady's Birthplace

Coventry, that do'st adorn
The country wherein I was born,
Yet therein lies not thy praise,
Why I should crown thy tow'rs with bays:
'Tis not thy wall[1] me to thee weds,
Thy ports, nor thy proud pyramids,
Nor thy trophies of the boar,[2]
But that she which I adore,
Which scarce goodness' self can pair,
First there breathing, blest, thy air;
    Idea, in which name I hide
Her, in my heart deifi'd,
For what good man's mind can see,

Only her Ideas be;
She, in whom the Virtues came
In woman's shape, and took her name,
She so far past imitation,
As but Nature our creation
Could not alter, she had aimed,
More than woman to have framed:
She, whose truly written story
To thy poor name shall add more glory
Than if it should have been thy chance
T'have bred our Kings that conquer'd France.

    Had she been born the former age,
That house had been a pilgrimage,
And reputed more divine
Than Walsingham or Becket's shrine.[3]

    That Princess,[4] to whom thou do'st owe
Thy freedom, whose clear blushing snow
The envious sun saw, when as she
Naked rode to make thee free,
Was but her type, as to foretell,
Thou should'st bring forth one, should excell
Her bounty, by whom thou should'st have
More honor than she freedom gave;
And that great Queen,[5] which but of late
Rul'd this land in peace and state,
Had not been, but Heaven had sworn,
A maid should reign, when she was born.

    Of thy streets, which thou hold'st best,
And most frequent of the rest,
Happy Mich-Park[6] ev'ry year,
On the fourth of August[7] there,
Let thy maids from Flora's bowers,
With their choice and daintiest flowers,
Deck thee up, and from their store,
With brave garlands crown that door.

    The old man passing by that way
To his son in time shall say,
"There was that lady born, which long
To after-ages shall be sung";
Who unawares, being passed by,
Back to that house shall cast his eye,
Speaking my verses as he goes,

And with a sigh shut ev'ry close.
    Dear city, travelling by thee,
When thy rising spires I see,
Destined her place of birth,
Yet me thinks the very earth
Hallowed is, so far as I
Can thee possibly decry:
Then thou, dwelling in this place,
Hearing some rude hind disgrace
Thy city with some scurvy thing,
Which some jester forth did bring,
Speak these lines where thou do'st come,
And strike the slave forever dumb.

Drayton's notes:
1. Coventry finely walled.
2. The shoulder-bone of a boar of mighty bigness.
3. Two famous pilgrimages, the one in Norfolk, the other in Kent.
4. Godiva, Duke Leofric's wife, who obtained the freedom of the city of her husband by riding through it naked.
5. Queen Elizabeth.
6. A noted street in Coventry.
7. His mistress' birthday.

To the Cambro-Britans and Their Harp, His Ballad of Agincourt

Fair stood the wind for France,
When we our sails advance,
Nor now to prove our chance,
Longer will tarry;
But putting to the main,
At Caux, the mouth of Seine,
With all his martial train,
Landed King Harry.

And taking many a fort,
Furnish'd in warlike sort,

Marcheth tow'rds Agincourt,
In happy hour;
Skirmishing day by day,
With those that stop'd his way,
Where the French gen'ral lay,
With all his power.

Which in the height of pride,
King HENRY to deride,
His ransom to provide
To the King sending,
Which he neglects the while,
As from a nation vile,
Yet with an angry smile,
Their fall portending.

And turning to his men,
Quoth our brave HENRY then,
Though they be one to ten,
Be not amazed.
Yet have we well begun,
Battles so bravely won,
Have ever to the sun
By fame been raised.

And for myself (quoth he),
This my full rest shall be,
England ne'r mourn for me,
Nor more esteem me.
Victor I will remain,
Or on this earth lie slain,
Never shall she sustain,
Loss to redeem me.

Poitiers and Crecy tell,
When most their pride did swell,
Under our swords they fell,
No less our skill is,
Than when our grandsire great,
Claiming the regal seat,
By many a warlike feat,
Lop'd the French lillies.

The Duke of York so dread
The eager vaward led;
With the main HENRY sped,
Amongst his henchmen.
EXCESTER had the rear,
A braver man not there,
O Lord how hot they were,
On the false Frenchmen!

They now to fight are gone,
Armor on armor shone,
Drum now to drum did groan,
To hear was wonder;
That with the cries they make
The very earth did shake,
Trumpet to trumpet spake,
Thunder to thunder.

Well it thine age became,
O noble ERPINGHAM,
Which didst the signal aim
To our hid forces;
When from a meadow by,
Like a storm suddenly,
The English archery
Struck the French horses.

With Spanish yew so strong,
Arrows a cloth-yard long,
That like to serpents stung,
Piercing the weather;
None from his fellow starts,
But playing manly parts,
And like true English hearts
Stuck close together.

When down their bows they threw,
And forth their bilboes drew,
And on the French they flew,
Not one was tardy;
Arms were from shoulders sent,

Scalps to the teeth were rent,
Down the French peasants went,
Our men were hardy.

This while our noble King,
His broad-sword brandishing,
Down the French host did ding,
As to o'erwhelm it;
And many a deep wound lent,
His arms with blood besprent,
And many a cruel dent
Bruised his helmet.

GLOSTER, that Duke so good,
Next to the royal blood,
For famous England stood,
With his brave brother;
CLARENCE, in steel so bright,
Though but a maiden knight,
Yet in that furious fight
Scarce such another.

WARWICK in blood did wade,
OXFORD the foe invade,
And cruel slaughter made,
Still as they ran up;
SUFFOLK his ax did ply,
BEAUMONT and WILLOUGHBY
Bare them right doughtily,
FERRERS and FANHOPE.

Upon Saint CRISPIN's day
Fought was this noble fray,
Which fame did not delay,
To England to carry;
O, when shall *English* men
With such acts fill a pen,
Or *England* breed again
Such a King HARRY?

Appendix B
Drayton and Ben Jonson

One of the main problems surrounding the relations between Drayton and Jonson lies in the interpretation of Jonson's eulogistic poem in the 1627 *Battle of Agincourt*, "The Vision of Ben Jonson on the Muses of His Friend M. Drayton." J. W. Hebel has argued that the poem is deliberately excessive in its praise of Drayton, in effect mocking him as Jonson and the other wits had mocked Thomas Coryat in their "commendations" of his *Crudities* (1611).[1] Jonson's only other explicit mention of Drayton appears in his *Conversations*, where he told Drummond that he "esteemed not" Drayton and that Drayton was afraid of him. Drummond also records some unkind comments on *Poly-Olbion* and other poems by Drayton. This evidence[2] would seem to deny any possibility of friendship between the two, at least at the time of the *Conversations* (January 1619).

To begin with, though, can we rely on the *Conversations* as a reliable index to Jonson's attitudes in 1627? Drummond's manuscript preserves a great many things said in an offhand way by a man who probably did not know his words were being remembered for posterity, and who by some accounts was given to blustering in his cups. I would prefer to rely mainly on "The Vision" itself in this matter, and on whatever can be inferred from other laudatory verses by Jonson. Such evidence shows the poem to be a typical Jonsonian tribute—excessive in its enthusiasm, perhaps, but not at all like the Coryat hoax, where the irony and ridicule are painfully obvious.

The opening lines of "The Vision" do broach the subject of friendship, but suggest neither estrangement nor enmity:

> "It hath been question'd, Michael, if I be
> A friend at all; or, if at all, to thee:
> Because, who make the question, have not seen
> Those ambling visits pass in verse between
> Thy Muse and mine, as they expect."

147

The first line-and-a-half merely says, "Some people wonder if I am capable of friendship at all," indicating that some readers may have questioned the sincerity of the author's many poems on his friends and on the special virtues of friendship. At this point Jonson turns to Drayton: "Or if I am a friend, am I yours?" But, the next three lines continue, such questions are only asked by people who suppose that friendship between poets requires the exchange of commendatory verses. He then admits:

> " . . . 'Tis true:
> You have not writ to me, nor I to you;
> And, though I now begin, 'tis not to rub
> Haunch against haunch, or raise a rhyming club
> About the town: this reck'ning I will pay,
> Without conferring symbols. This's my day."

If Jonson were writing to insult Drayton, he would not (as he does in the first five lines of this passage) begin with this frank disclaimer against "rhyming clubs," a species of arty togetherness that we may be sure Jonson deplored. The commercial image of the last two lines is ambiguous: to confer symbols means to compare contributions (a defunct sense of "symbol" is the portion donated to a picnic or feast) and to compare figures on a written bill of sale (hence "reck'ning"). Jonson says that he will make the tribute with liberality—that it is his "day" to pick up the tab.

This metaphor of liberality sets the hyperbolic tone for the poem, and indeed the aging Ben pulls out all the stops. He says that he found *Idea* to be "pure and perfect poesy," that he wept over *The Miseries of Queen Margaret*, and that the songs of *Poly-Olbion* "ravish'd" him! A bit much, perhaps—yet is this not precisely the tone of Jonson's poem "To the Memory of My Beloved, the Author William Shakespeare?" We do not see any irony in "Soul of the Age! / The applause! delight! the wonder of the stage!" We ourselves would say something of this sort about Shakespeare, so we naturally take these lines to mean what they say. Yet Jonson is more often moved by the rhetorical demands of his poetry of praise than by the actual worth of the subject. An epideictic poem was supposed to be written in the grand style, and in Jonson the line between grand and grandiose is not always observed. He is almost comically overwhelmed by Selden's learning in "An Epistle to Master John Selden":

> "I yield, I yield, the matter of your praise
> Flows in upon me, and I cannot raise

A bank against it. Nothing but the round
Large clasp of Nature such a wit can bound.
Monarch in Letters!"

Repeatedly, it will be found, such hyperbole is inseparable from the act
of praise in Jonson's poetry. He is able to salute Richard Lord Weston
as: "That waking man! that eye of state! / Who seldom sleeps! whom
bad men only hate!" At times the hyperbole is downright silly if we
read it in a literal-minded spirit: observe his commendation of the Earl
of Newcastle's stables:

". . . when I saw the floor, and room,
I look'd for Hercules to be the groom:
And cri'd, away with the Caesarian bread,
At these immortal mangers Virgil fed."

As I see it, by its very frequency, hyperbole, no matter how extravagant,
cannot be relied upon as a clue to irony in Jonson's epideictic poetry.

On the face of it, moreover, several of the judgments passed in "A
Vision" demand a straightforward reading. Jonson's particular enthusiasm over *The Battle of Agincourt* has already been mentioned in my
discussion of that work. Other comments on the poems of the 1627
volume suggest Jonson's unqualified approval:

"But then refreshed, with thy Faerie Court,
I look on Cynthia and Sirena's sport,
As, on two flow'ry carpets, that did rise,
And with their grassy green restor'd mine eyes.
Yet give me leave to wonder at the birth
Of thy strange Moon-Calf, both thy strain of mirth,
And Gossip-got acquaintance, as, to us
Thou hadst brought Lapland, or old Cobalus,
Empusa, Lamia, or some monster, more
Than Africk knew, or the full Grecian state!"

Finally, it should be noted that none of the poems praised in the first
two-thirds of "The Vision" was actually included in the 1627 volume.
This means that Jonson's poem is substantially a commendation of all
Drayton's work—a formal affirmation that the two leading exemplars of
the public mode in early seventeenth-century poetry, the two most frequently called "laureates," were in sympathy. All in all, "The Vision"
is quite a good advertisement for Drayton, and I can find no irony in it
directed against him. Whether Jonson actually read all of the poems he
praises may be questioned, but that is another matter.

On Drayton's part Jonson is mentioned only in the brief tribute in the elegy to Reynolds, which Hebel finds rather cold and impersonal:

"Next these, learn'd Jonson in this list I bring,
Who had drunk deep of the Pierian spring,
Whose knowledge did him worthily prefer,
And long was Lord here of the theater,
Who in opinion made our learn'st to stick,
Whether in poems rightly dramatic,
Strong Seneca or Plautus, he or they,
Should bear the Buskin or the Sock away."

These lines depict Jonson in the roles so often given him by his friends and admirers—as monarch of the theater, as a man of great learning, and as the dramatist who did most to classicize the English stage. The tone is no more impersonal than that of other tributes in this section of the elegy, which is devoted to the major figures of Drayton's generation (ll. 105–36). The truth is, as Jonson hinted at the beginning of "The Vision," that he and Drayton traveled in quite different circles. If the anecdote about the "merry meeting" with Shakespeare is true (see Newdigate, p. 141), it was probably their mutual acquaintance with Shakespeare that brought the two poets together on that occasion.

This is not to say that they exercise their art in the same way, or that they were fully in sympathy politically. Both of them share with Spenser the Platonic poet's tendency toward allegory. But whereas in Spenser the allegorical vehicle is myth (Diana or St. George, for example), Drayton's vehicle is characteristically historical, while Jonson's figures are the notable persons of his own time. Drayton's "heroes" are history-becoming-myth, history idealized—Henry II embodies the truth of obsessive, illicit love; Mortimer, of lust for power; Surrey, of cultural virtuosity. Topical allusion has a special place in this poetry as in Spenser's, for all historical figures are but manifestations of the eternal types. Piers Gaveston shares the same insidious parasitism as his counterpart at the court of James or Elizabeth; but he does so more completely, so that men who know the type in poetry are better able to see the flesh-and-blood courtier as he "really" is. As Sidney says, the poet brings forth "forms such as never were in Nature," a "golden" world rather than the "brazen" one of nature: as gold is to brass, so the refined virtues or vices of Surrey and Gaveston stand in relation to the actual courtiers of Drayton's time.[3]

Ben Jonson adopts still another course in his poetry, where the vehicle is neither myth nor history, but contemporary society. When Jonson speaks of his epigrams as pictures,[4] he is thinking of them in a sense not unlike Sidney's in the example of the "more excellent" painter, who is compared to the "right poet": "who, having no law but wit, bestow[s] that in colors upon you which is fittest for the eye to see: as the constant though lamenting look of Lucrecia, when she punished in herself another's fault; wherein he painteth not Lucrecia, whom he never saw, but painteth the outward beauty of such a virtue."[5] The poem "To Mary Lady Wroth" ("Madam, had all antiquity been lost") poses an interesting contrast between the mythological inclination of Spenser and the topical approach of Jonson. Lady Wroth is associated with Ceres, Oenone, Flora, May, Diana, and Pallas—all aspects of the ideal country noblewoman—so that "had all antiquity been lost" men would still be able to know these virtues through her. In the *Epistles* Drayton had converted mythological types into persons of English history; now we find Jonson bringing the types into his own society.

This tendency is akin to the Platonic element in Jonson's masques, which amount to Platonic ceremonies in which the natural and artistic versions of the eternal are momentarily fused in the persons of the spectacle. Like his poems, his masques are not mere flattery (with some exceptions, of course; even Platonic poets are human), but attempts to capture truth, beauty, and goodness as they are bodied forth in the great personalities of his society. Chances are, we could not recognize any of these personalities in his masques and poems merely by dint of Jonson's descriptions and commendations, so generalized are they and so abstracted from the world of experience. Nevertheless, among all the Platonic poets Jonson came nearest to bridging the inevitable rift between the two worlds of experience and art.

This brief discussion should at least make it evident that the comparison of Jonson and Drayton cannot take place apart from a wider context, which was not properly in the domain of my book. Jonson seems to have been unable to follow Drayton as a historical poet, even though he may have wanted to at some part of his career. He told Drummond that he planned to write an epic on the worthies of England, to be called "Heroölogia"; also, at his death he left behind extensive plans for a play on the fall of Mortimer. His inability or disinclination to write historical verse parallels his early rejection of mythological verse,[6] for he was, after all, very much a man of the new age. Jonson was as strongly affected by the immediacy of experience as were Donne and the other writers of the contemporary theater, so that he could not abandon the world of sense as wholeheartedly as had Spenser—or as halfheartedly as Drayton.

Notes

Abbreviations used in the notes:

C.S.P.D.: Calendar of State Papers, Domestic Series
EHR: English Historical Review
HLQ: Huntington Library Quarterly
JEGP: Journal of English and Germanic Philology
JWCI: Journal of the Warburg and Courtauld Institute
MLR: Modern Language Review
PBA: Proceedings of the British Academy
PQ: Philological Quarterly
SCN: Seventeenth-Century News
SP: Studies in Philology
SQ: Shakespeare Quarterly
TLS: [London] Times Literary Supplement

CHAPTER 1: PRELIMINARIES

1. In Robert Gray's sermon *A Good Speed to Virginia* (1609), the Virginia colonists are compared to the children of Joseph taking leave of Joshua (Joshua 17:14), while unemployed (or, as he calls them, "idle") Englishmen who remain at home are likened to the sons of Jacob: "And Jacob, seeing his sons destitute of counsel in this extremity, did sharply reprehend them for the dissolute managing of their present state, saying: 'Why gaze ye upon one another, Behold, I have heard that there is food in Egypt; get ye down thither, and buy us food thence, that we may live.' Even so it may be with a company of people in this land, which do nothing but gaze one upon another, destitute of counsel, advice, and means, how to provide justly for their maintenance. They hear of honorable projects abroad, . . . of plenty and abundance of many good things, of which a fruitful country largely makes offer unto them . . . yet they still sit following their intemperance, incontinence, and other luxurious and

riotous courses, to the high dishonor of almighty God." These are the "loitering hinds" of the first stanza of Drayton's ode. A more secular propagandist, Captain John Smith, found the biblical comparison a persuasive device with which to end his *Description of New England*: "But to conclude, Adam and Eve did first begin this innocent work, to plant the earth to remain to posterity, but not without labor, trouble and industry. Noah and his family began again the second plantation; and their seed as it still increased hath still planted new countries, and one country another: and so the world to that estate it is. But not without much hazard, travail, discontents and many disasters."

2. G. M. Trevelyan, *Illustrated English Social History* (London: Longmans, Green, 1951), II, 67, writes: "The attempt made during the Hundred Years' War to reduce France to an English province had been the first instinctive gesture of an awakening national consciousness and a new-felt power to expand. . . . This time the 'good yeoman whose limbs were made in England' went forth again, but not with chivalry and not under the King, but with an axe and plough to found a new civilization in the wilderness."

3.   "These lyric pieces, short, and few,
   Most worthy sir, I send to you,
   To read them be not weary:
   They may become John Hewes his lyre,
   Which oft at Polesworth by the fire
   Hath made us gravely merry."

4. Drayton is especially partial to the Welsh, or Cambro-Britains, in *Poly-Olbion* on account of their pure "British" stock. For some suggestions about the influence of the tradition of *beirdh* or Welsh bard on Drayton, see P. G. Buchloh, *Michael Drayton* (Neumünster: K. Wachholtz, 1964), pp. 77 ff.

5. The error still persists in some quarters (e.g., *Chambers's Biographical Dictionary*, 1961 ed.) that this work was called in by the authorities, even though R. B. McKerrow demonstrated in 1910 that this could not have been so. See *Works*, V, 271.

6. See *The Second Part of the Return from Parnassus* (1606), I.ii:
   "Drayton's sweet muse is like a sanguine dye,
   Able to ravish the rash gazer's eye."
"However he wants one true note of a Poet of our times, and that is this, that he cannot swagger it well in a Tavern nor domineer in a hothouse."

7. Bauzen's skin is badger skin; Cordiwin, Spanish leather; meniveere or miniver, a white ceremonial fur.

8. Echoes of this piece can be heard in the later song from *The Shepherd's Sirena*, as in this stanza from the third eclogue:
   "Range all thy swans, fair Thames, together on a rank,
   And place them duly one by one upon thy stately bank,
   Then set together all agood
   Recording to the silver flood,
   And crave the tuneful nightingale to help you with her lay,
   The osel and the throstlecock, chief music of our may."
   and the refrain from "The Shepherd's Sirena":
   "On thy bank,
   In a rank,
   Let thy swans sing her,
   And with their music,
   along let them bring her."

9. Hallett Smith, *Elizabethan Poetry* (Cambridge, Mass.: Harvard Univ. Press, 1952), pp. 103 ff.

10. Cf. *Gaveston*, ll. 613–18 and 1267–72. For a possible solution to the problem of Gaveston's eternal reward, see Tillyard, *Shakespeare's History Plays* (1944; rpt. Harmondsworth: Penguin, 1964), p. 74, where it is noted that Buckingham and other noblemen in the *Mirror* are all portrayed in hell, but to the objection that hell is hardly a suitable place for all of them, Baldwin replies that "hell" simply means the grave.

11. See the tribute to these three in the epilogue to *Endimion and Phoebe,* ll. 993–1004.

12. See the commendatory poem "To my worthy friend Mr. George Chapman" in Chapman's translation of Hesiod's *Georgics* (1618).

13. Fulgentius, *Mitologiarum libri tres* II.xvi. The same interpretation occurs in the ancient scholia on Appollonius' *Argonautica* IV.57.

14. Boccaccio, *Genealogiae Deorum* IV.xvi (43b); Comes, *Mythologiae* (Venice, 1581): "Alii dicunt primum Endymionem rerum sublimum speculationem invenisse, cui rei fabulae locum dedit luna ob tam varias luminis formas & mutationes, cum de illa praecipue cognoscenda esset sollicitus: qui cum noctu his considerationibus esset intentus, somno non fruebatur, at dormiebat per diem" (p. 222).

15. Drayton published a doctored-up satiric version, *The Man in the Moon*, in 1606, but the operation was not a success. Like the revised *Gaveston* and *Matilda*, it may be seen as a last effort to capitalize on a bad investment.

16. An excellent argument for Metaphysical influence is presented by Rosemond Tuve, *Elizabethan and Metaphysical Imagery* (1947; rpt. Chicago: Univ. of Chicago Press, 1965), pp. 62–76. See also Jörg

Schönert, "Draytons Sonett-Revisionen," *Anglia*, 85 (1967), 161–83.

17. Elegy "To Henry Reynolds," ll. 86–89. Cf. Drayton's Elegy for Sidney in the fourth eclogue of *The Shepherd's Garland*.

18. " 'Fantastickly I Sing': Drayton's *Idea* of 1619," *SP*, 66 (1969), 204–16.

19. Lawrence Stone, *The Crisis of the Aristocracy* (London: Oxford Univ. Press, 1965), p. 391.

20. Perez Zagorin, "The Court and the Country," *EHR*, 77 (1962), notes that a member of parliament in 1625 prided himself on being "neither Courtier nor Lawyer but a plain Country Gentleman." Cf. Nicholas Breton, *The Court and the Country* (1618). The conflict is surveyed expansively in Zagorin's *The Court and the Country* (New York: Atheneum, 1970).

21. Compare his various panegyrics to King Charles and Buckingham with his tribute "To the most learned, wise, and Arch-Antiquary, Master John Selden." Selden, of course, was a leader in the anti-Royalist faction of parliament.

22. Seventh *Nemean* ode. See Rosemary Harriott, *Poetry and Criticism before Plato* (London: Methuen, 1969), chap. i.

23. Homer Nearing, Jr., *English Historical Poetry 1599–1641* (Philadelphia, 1945), p. 24.

24. See H. R. Trevor-Roper, "The Last Elizabethan" and "Social Causes of the Great Rebellion," in *Historical Essays* (1957; rpt. New York: Harper Torchbooks, 1966), pp. 107, 203; Roy C. Strong, "The Popular Celebration of the Accession Day of Queen Elizabeth I," *JWCI*, 21 (1958), 86–103. Strong reports that when the Long Parliament met on 17 November 1640, the anniversary of Elizabeth's accession, it was urged to "make this another blessed seventeenth of November" (p. 103).

CHAPTER 2: LESSONS OF THE PAST

1. Herschel Baker, *The Race of Time* (Toronto: Univ. of Toronto Press, 1967), p. 20.

2. Cf. Giovanni Pontano, *Actius*, in *I dialoghi*, ed. C. Previtera (Florence: Sansoni, 1943), p. 193: "Eam [sc. history] maiores nostri quandam quasi solutam poeticam putavere, recteque ipsi quidem: pleraque enim habent inter se communia: ut rerum vetustarum ac remotarum repetitiones, ut locorum, populorum, nationum, gentium descriptiones, quin etiam illorum situs, mores, leges, consuetudines,

ut vitiorum insectationes, virtutum ac benefactorum laudes. . . . Itaque neutrius magis quam alterius aut propositum est aut studium ut doceat, delectet, moveat, ut etiam prosit, rem apparet eamque ante oculos ponat, ac nunc extollat aliud nunc aliud elevet." I owe my acquaintance with Quattrocento writings on history to a lecture by Professor Hanna Gray of Northwestern University. For an English "apology for history," see T. H. Blackburn, "Edmund Bolton's *The Cabanet Royal*," *Studies in the Renaissance*, 14 (1967), 159–71.

3. F. J. Levy, *Tudor Historical Thought* (San Marino, Calif.: Huntington Library, 1967), p. 293.

4. Quoted in Baker, *Race of Time*, p. 45.

5. On the use of orations, see Leonard F. Dean, *Tudor Theories of History Writing*, U. of Mich. Contrib. in Modern Philology, 1 (Ann Arbor, 1947).

6. William Baldwin, epilogue to Sackville's "The Complaint of Henry Duke of Buckingham," in *The Mirror for Magistrates*, ed. Lily B. Campbell (1938; rpt. New York: Barnes and Noble, 1960), p. 346.

7. *Annals*, pp. 339–40.

8. *Annals*, p. 343, and *Barons' Wars* V.46.

9. Preface, *History of the World* in *Works* (1829; rpt. New York: Burt Franklin, n.d.), II, xlii.

10. See Baker, *Race of Time*, p. 64. Drayton subordinates Fate to Providence at the end of his *Moses*, when commenting on the apparent calamity of the patriarch's death before reaching Canaan:

    "So wisely worketh that eternal Being

    By the still changes of [men's] varying state,

    (As to the end through the beginning seeing)

    To build the frame of unavoided fate."

    Explaining how the deluge was brought on by the conjunction of the planets, Drayton says in *Noah's Flood* that "God makes the stars his instruments to punish the wicked" (*Works*, III, 343).

11. Lily B. Campbell, "The Use of Historical Patterns in the Reign of Elizabeth," *HLQ*, 1 (1938), 135–67.

12. *History of the World, ed. cit.*, II, xlii.

13. *The Civil Wars* I.61.

14. Nietzsche develops the notion of monumental, as opposed to antiquarian and critical, history in his *Thoughts out of Season*.

15. See K. Tillotson, *Works*, V, 41.

16. *Mortimeriados*, l. 1491. The relevant lines, including the description of the London plague, are 1464–1617.

17. "The Vision of Ben Jonson," l. 44, in *Works*, III, 4.

18. Cf. John Buxton, ed. *Michael Drayton* (London: Muses' Library,

1953), II, 707–8. Mrs. Tillotson (*Works*, V, 42) admits that *Mortimeriados* "has an enchantment which is lacking in the more responsible and competent" *Barons' Wars*.

19. Drayton's reasons for adopting ottava rima over rhyme royal are prosodically impressionistic: "For the stanza of seven first named, the quadrin doth never double, or to use a word of heraldry, never bringeth forth gemels. The quinzain too soon. The sestin hath twins in the base, but they detain not the music nor the close (as musicians term it) long enough for an epic poem. This of eight both holds the tune clean through to the base of the column (which is the couplet, the foot or bottom) and closeth not but with a full satisfaction to the ear for so long detention" (*Works*, II, 4).

20. Cf. *Mortimeriados*, ll. 120 ff. and *Barons' Wars* I.24; *Mort.*, ll. 149 ff. and *B.W.* I.34; *Mort.*, ll. 169 ff. and *B.W.* I.36; *Mort.* ll. 239 ff. and *B.W.* I.64.

21. *C.S.P.D.*, 1619–1623, p. 237.

22. Lawrence Stone, *Crisis of the Aristocracy*, pp. 72–73.

23. *Deplorable Life* (1628), st. 10. This edition was supposedly published without Hubert's consent; an authorized one appeared the next year.

24. One topical reference in the Edward-Gaveston-Mortimer story may be to the troubles between James VI and the Duke of Lennox: this is the reading of Marlowe's *Edward II* offered by J. M. Berdan, "Marlowe's *Edward II*," *PQ*, 3 (1924), 197–207. Quite possibly the vogue of literature about Richard II and Edward II partly arose at the prospect of the effete King's coming to the English throne, though so far as I know no one has ever advanced this view.

25. Drayton himself notes the epistle from King John to Matilda as an exception to this rule, in that it is "much more poetical than historical, making no mention at all of the occurents of time or state." Yet even this unconcernedness, he adds, is historically accurate, "rightly fashioning the humour of this King as hath been truly noted by the most authentical writers."

26. *Shakespeare's History Plays*, pp. 81–82.

27. The ratio is 1:7, whereas in the Queen Mary and Charles Brandon pair, for example, it is 1:65.

28. Stow, *Annals of England* (1592), p. 299. Drayton's gloss on this passage only compounds the felony: "Roger Mortimer, called the great Lord Mortimer, grandfather to this Roger, which was afterward the first Earl of March, erected again the Round Table at Kenilworth, after the ancient order of King Arthur's Table, with the retinue of an hundred knights and an hundred ladies in his house,

for the entertaining of such adventurers as came thither from all parts of Christendom." In Holinshed, Roger Mortimer's game (at Killingworth *again*) is mentioned, but it is not called the Round Table, nor is it in any other way associated with Arthur.

29. *Works*, II, 130.

30. Ll. 57–60. Drayton's note: "Few Queens of England or France were ever more princely allied than this Queen, as hath been noted by historiographers."

31. Ll. 47–50. The theme of divine foreordination is also expounded in ll. 29–40.

32. Drayton's note: "A prophecy of Queen Mary's barrenness, and of the happy and glorious reign of Queen Elizabeth; her restoring of religion, the abolishing of the Romish servitude, and casting aside the yoke of Spain."

33. Thomas Wilson, *The State of England* (1600), rpt. in *Camden Miscellany*, 16 (1936), 2.

34. Wilson remarks on the Seymours' claim: "It is certain that Charles Brandon their grandfather, when he married Mary, had another wife called the Lady Anne Mortimer, who lived after the other" (*State of England*, p. 6).

35. See Newdigate, pp. 128–30, where another cause is suggested. The controversy over Elizabeth's succession seems also to have been matter for the stage. See Gertrude C. Reese, "The Question of the Succession in Elizabethan Drama," *Texas Studies in English*, 22 (1942), 59–85. *Sir Thomas Wyat* is one of several plays that Reese sees as advancing the Suffolk claim (pp. 73–75).

36. *The Anatomy of Melancholy* III.2.3.

37. *Works*, II, 252.

38. See Jean Gagen, "Love and Honor in Dryden's Heroic Plays," *PMLA*, 77 (1962), 208–20; Mark Rose, *Heroic Love: Studies in Sidney and Spenser* (Cambridge, Mass.: Harvard Univ. Press, 1968).

39. See my article, "Convention and Design in Drayton's *Heroicall Epistles*," *PMLA*, 83 (1968), 35–41.

40. Anthony LaBranche, "Drayton's *Barons Warres* and the Rhetoric of Historical Poetry," *JEGP*, 62 (1963), 82–95.

41. Cf. Robert Langbaum, *The Poetry of Experience* (1957; rpt. New York: Norton, 1963). Drayton's epistles more nearly approach "reflective poetry" (p. 38) than "the poetry of experience," in which "the poem is an authentic experience which gives birth to an idea rather than the illustration of a ready-made idea" (p. 48). The distinction is useful, though I question the bias of "authentic" and "ready-made."

42. *English Literature in the Sixteenth Century Excluding Drama* (London: Oxford Univ. Press, 1954), p. 526.
43. Kathleen Tillotson, "Michael Drayton as a 'Historian' in the Legend of Cromwell," *MLR*, 34 (1939), p. 200; also introduction in *Works*, V, 167–70.
44. In a copy of *Cromwell* a seventeenth-century reader has written "papist" beside Drayton's name (*Works*, V, 170).
45. Mario Praz, *Storia della letteratura inglese* (Florence: Sansoni, 1964), expresses this opinion, calling the Elizabethan period "a first *Sturm und Drang* in Europe" (p. 81).

CHAPTER 3: ANTIQUARIANISM AND RENEWAL

1. I can understand anyone's reluctance even to pick up a volume of 15,000 alexandrines—providing he does not plan to write about the poem. Henry Hallam, *Introduction to the Literature of Europe*, described it as "a poem of about 30,000 lines in length" (quoted in Moulton's *Library of Literary Criticism*, I, 704). Perhaps on this authority A. L. Rowse, *The England of Elizabeth* (New York: Macmillan, 1951), says that the poem "ambles along for 30,000 lines" (p. 60). This is at least an improvement on Alan Burgess, *Warwickshire* (London: R. Hale, 1950), who writes that Drayton's "most famous work is the thirty thousand word epic called *Polyolbion*, which is much too long to read" (p. 294).
2. *Poly-Olbion* VI.275–98; X.276–79; I.312; I.194–203. Selden, in his notes, is usually quite critical of legendary history by comparison with Drayton: on Brutus, see *Works*, IV, 21.
3. Lewis F. Ball, "The Background of the Minor English Renaissance Epics," *ELH*, 1 (1934), p. 87.
4. *Poly-Olbion* XIII.282 ff. On contemporary topographical literature, see Jack B. Oruch, "Topography in the Prose and Poetry of the English Renaissance, 1540–1640," Unpubl. diss. (Indiana Univ., 1964).
5. Ray Heffner, Jr., "Michael Drayton as a Pastoral Poet," Unpubl. diss. (Yale Univ., 1953), p. 219.
6. 14 April 1619. Quoted in Newdigate, p. 161.
7. Bent Juel-Jensen, "Bibliography," in *Works*, V, 301.
8. P. G. Buchloh, *Michael Drayton*, p. 227. My discussion of Part II is highly influenced by his, pp. 223–34.
9. *Works*, IV, 391.
10. *Ariosto, Shakespeare and Corneille*, trans. D. Ainslie (New York: H. Holt, 1920), pp. 202–3.

11. ". . . I heare again, thy Drum to beat
    A better cause, and strike the bravest heate
    That ever yet did fire the English blood!
    Our right in France! if ritely understood.
    There thou art Homer! Pray thee, use the style
    Thou hast deserved" ("The Vision of Ben Jonson," in *Works*,
    III, 4).
12. *Iliad* XXIV.468–69 (tr. Chapman).
13. C. D. Penn, *The Navy under the Early Stuarts* (London: J. Hogg,
    1920), p. 174.
14. Newdigate, p. 210.
15. *History of the Rebellion* I.86.
16. *Ibid.* I.84–85. The notion that England suffered from a surfeit of
    peace also appears in Jonson's "Epistle to a Friend, to Persuade Him
    to the Wars," written in the earlier 1620s.
17. Newdigate, p. 219, quotes the antiquary William Fulman, who de-
    scribes Drayton's funeral cortege as "reaching in order by two and
    two, from his lodging almost to the Strandbridge"—a distance of at
    least three or four city blocks, as I read the map. Thomas Fuller,
    The Worthies of England, ed. J. Freeman (London: G. Allen and
    Unwin, 1952), wrote of Drayton, "He was a pious poet, his con-
    science having always the command of his fancy, very temperate in
    his life, slow of speech, and inoffensive in company" (p. 590).

CHAPTER 4: THE DISORDER OF THE PRESENT

1. Dick Taylor, "Drayton and the Countess of Bedford," *SP*, 49 (1952),
   214–28.
2. This is contrary to received opinion. Cf. David Mathew, *The Jacobean Age* (London: Longmans, Green, 1938): "Certainly it seems
   improbable that any contemporary, who was out of touch with the
   politics of favouritism, could ever have successfully understood *The
   Owle* or plowed past the fauna in that privileged jungle" (p. 106).
   See notes by Tillotson and later findings in J. Buxton, ed., *Michael
   Drayton*, I, 291–94, for the decipherings of two early seventeenth-
   century readers.
3. C. G. Cruickshank, *Elizabeth's Army*, 2nd ed. (Oxford: Clarendon
   Press, 1966), pp. 183–88.
4. Cf. Barnaby Rich, *Faults, Faults, and Nothing Else but Faults*
   (1606): "A proud Court makes a lean country" (p. 55).

5. Newdigate errs, I think, in placing the cause of Drayton's hostility in "Drayton's discontent at failing to receive due recognition for his poetry" (p. 132); he does not entertain the possibility that Drayton is representative of a reactionary trend.

6. For the evidence, see Newdigate, chap. ix.

7. Lawrence Stone, *Crisis of the Aristocracy*, pp. 72–74, 92. The quotation is from *C.S.P.D.* 1619–1623, p. 253. Later, Parliamentarians like Francis Osborne saw this as a chief disgrace of the realm: "the honor of knighthood, which Antiquity preserved sacred, as the cheapest and readiest jewel to present virtue with, was promiscuously laid on any head belonging to the yeomandry (made addle through pride and contempt of their ancestral pedigree) that had but a Court friend" (*Historical Memoirs*, in *Works* [London, 1701], p. 421).

8. D. H. Willson, *King James VI and I* (New York: Holt, 1956), pp. 190–191; *The Chamberlain Letters*, ed. E. M. Thomas (London: Murray, 1966), p. 130.

9. Peyton, *The Divine Catastrophe of the Kingly Family of the House of Stuarts* (1652; rpt., London, 1731), pp. 3–23. Sir Simonds D'Ewes wrote, "Most men execrated the name and memory of George Villiers, Duke of Buckingham, whom they conceived to be the bitter root and fountain of all their mischief" (*Autobiography*, quoted in David Mathew, *The Jacobean Age*, p. 291). Upon his assassination in 1628, a popular lampoon described Buckingham as:

"The courtier's bane, the countries' hate,
An agent for the Spanish state;
The Romists' friend, the gospel's foe,
The Church and Kingdom's overthrow."

For similar pronouncements, see F. W. Fairholt, ed., *Poems and Songs Relating to George Villiers, Duke of Buckingham*, Percy Soc. Repr. (London, 1850).

10. Cf. Willson, *King James VI and I*, p. 421: In the debate, "Member after member pointed to Spain as the great enemy abroad and to the Catholics as the great menace in England. Let the war be against Spain, not merely by pottering in the Palatinate but by attacking Spain and the Indies on land and sea in true Elizabethan fashion."

11. G. Davies, *The Early Stuarts* (Oxford: Oxford Univ. Press, 1937), p. 22; *C.S.P.D.* 1619–1623, pp. 153, 158, 169. See Louis B. Wright, "Propaganda against James I's 'Appeasement' of Spain," *HLQ*, 6 (1943), 149–72, and the anonymous pamphlet *Tom Tell-Troath* (1622; rpt. in *Complaint and Reform in England*, ed. S. Pargellis and W. H. Dunham [New York: Octagon, 1968]).

12. Reynolds, *Votivae Angliae* (1624), D4^v.

13. Cf. Chamberlain on the possibility of Charles' marriage to the Cathlic Infanta: "Some spare not to say that all goes backward since this connivance in religion came in, both in our wealth, valor, honor, and reputation, and that it is visibly seen that God blesses nothing we take in hand, whereas in Queen Elizabeth's time, who stood firm in God's cause, all things did flourish" (*The Chamberlain Letters*, p. 355). This nostalgia continues well into the period of the rebellion. Osborne saw Elizabeth's rule as an era "the felicity of which was never since matched, nor have we had yet any cause to hope it will be" (*Historical Memoirs*, p. 360). Cf. above, Chap. 1, n. 24.

14. *The Owl*, ll. 695–746. Also see the newly added lines 1059–64, in which the Eagle inexplicably vanishes, leaving the Owl to govern things "for the great good of the public Weal." Here the Owl represents the wisdom of commons, the power of men (at least some men) to govern themselves, a notion often defended by Selden. Drayton, the feudal-minded monarchist, may have been groping toward some form of republicanism in his later years, but none is ever fully formulated.

15. Newdigate does not mention Hugh Drayton's case, but the person named must have been Drayton's uncle: cf. Newdigate, p. 226, and *C.S.P.D.* 1619–1623, p. 187.

16. Newdigate, p. 195.

17. Newdigate, pp. 201–2; Willson, *The Privy Councillors in the House of Commons* (Minneapolis: Univ. of Minnesota Press, 1940), p. 158 (Sackville had earlier disgraced himself with James by dueling, an event which Drayton's editors conjecture lies behind *The Shepherd's Sirena*). In 1610 Selden and his "chamber fellow" Edward Heyward wrote commendatory verses to Drayton's *Poems*. Another friend of Selden's, John Vaughan, wrote some enthusiastic lines for *The Battle of Agincourt* in 1627. Both Heyward and Vaughan were later executors of Selden's will.

18. Willson, *King James VI and I*, pp. 280–81; Osborne, *Historical Memoirs*, pp. 424, 434; D'Ewes, *Autobiography*, quoted in Mathew, *The Jacobean Age*, pp. 82–83; Newdigate, p. 160. K. Tillotson, "Drayton, Browne, and Wither," *TLS*, Nov. 27, 1937, p. 911, reports that at least four members of Drayton's circle, William Browne, George Wither, John Davies, and Christopher Brooke, received grants from Prince Henry but not from the Court. William Drummond's first published verses were among the elegies on the prince's death. There is thus some evidence that Henry (who was a well-known admirer of his father's enemy Ralegh) was becoming the

center of a "rival" court, including a set of poets quite different from the courtly followers of Jonson and Donne, such as Thomas Carew.

19. Philip J. Finkelpearl, *John Marston of the Middle Temple* (Cambridge, Mass.: Harvard Univ. Press, 1969) discusses the Inns as centers of opposition to the Court, but his outline is necessarily sketchy (pp. 62–69, 220–37). See also Stone, *Crisis of the Aristocracy*, pp. 690–91, and Kenneth Charlton, "Liberal Education and the Inns of Court in the Sixteenth Century," *British Journal of Educational Studies*, 9 (1960–1961), 25–38. These authorities make it clear that those who entered the Inns at this time did not necessarily do so to obtain a legal education, and strongly suggest that the rural gentry was more likely to educate its scions at the Inns than the universities. The present Librarian of the Inner Temple, Mr. W. W. S. Breem, has suggested to me that Drayton may have roomed at the Temple with one of its regular members, such being familiar practice in later years, and perhaps already at this time.

CHAPTER 5: POETRY AND THE PUBLIC MORALITY

1. "To His Friend the Author."
2. See comparisons in *Works*, V, 206, and Douglas Bush, *Mythology and The Renaissance Tradition* (1932; rev. ed. New York: Norton, 1963), p. 166.
3. On Drayton as a student of nature, see Thomas P. Harrison, "Drayton's Herbals," *Univ. of Texas Studies in English*, 23 (1943), 15–25, and *They Tell of Birds* (Austin: Univ. of Texas Press, 1956), pp. 109–31. Newdigate, *Works*, V, 232, lists 14 passages in *Poly-Olbion* and elsewhere that lament the ruin of the forests. Stone, *Crisis of the Aristocracy*, pp. 345–46, estimates that at this time the iron industry was consuming up to 20,000 acres of woodland a year. Drayton's complaint was shared by many contemporaries, e.g., Arthur Standish, *The Commons' Complaint* (on "the general destruction and waste of woods in this kingdom"), and R. C., *An Old Thrift Newly Revised*. Both works appeared in 1612, the year of *Poly-Olbion*.
4. See L. C. Knights, *Drama and Society in the Age of Jonson* (New York: G. W. Stewart, n. d.), chap. iii.
5. Rous, *Oil of Scorpions*, pp. 173–75; Fitzgeffrey, *Certain Elegies*, f. F2; *Hic Mulier*, f. A4ᵛ; *Haec Vir*, f. C2ᵛ; Osborne, *Historical Memoirs*, p. 429. On male-female fashions, cf. William Prynne, *The Unloveliness of Love Locks* (1628).

6. In current slang, the "town bull" meant "the most notable fornicator and womanizer in a village or township." Eric Partridge, *Shakespeare's Bawdy* (1947; rev. ed., London: Routledge & Kegan Paul, 1967), p. 203.

7. "Service" often denoted sexual activity; a pillion is a woman's saddle; a safeguard is an outer skirt worn by women to protect clothes while riding.

8. See the verses in *Works* by John Reynolds (III, 7; IV, 396); Beaumont (III, 355); Browne (IV, 393); Wither (IV, 394–96); Drummond's letter of 1618 in Newdigate, p. 179; Henry Reynolds' comment in *Mythomystes* (*Works*, V, xxx). For Drayton's own remarks on his critics, his "censures," and his neglect, see the preface to *Poly-Olbion*, Part II, and to *The Muses' Elysium*; also the elegies to Sandys and Jeffreys.

9. Stone, *Crisis of the Aristocracy*, pp. 662–68.

10. The notes, by Richard Butcher, are given in J. Buxton, ed., *Michael Drayton*, 291–94. On Drayton and the city, cf. above, Chap. 1, n. 3.

11. Perez Zagorin, "The Court and the Country," *EHR*, 77 (1962), 306–11.

12. Valerie Pearl, *London and the Outbreak of the Puritan Revolution* (London: Oxford Univ. Press, 1961), demonstrates that "London was more sympathetic to the crown than to Parliament in the national crisis of 1641" (p. 276).

13. L. C. Knights, "Shakespeare's Politics," *PBA*, 43 (1957), p. 124. The point has been more forcefully if more frenetically argued in D. N. Friesner, "William Shakespeare, Conservative," *SQ*, 20 (1969), 165–78.

14. Philip Styles, "Politics and Historical Research in the Early Seventeenth Century," in L. Fox, ed., *English Historical Scholarship in the Sixteenth and Seventeenth Centuries* (London: Oxford Univ. Press, 1956), 49–72; Willson, *James VI and I*, p. 297; Baker, *Race of Time*, p. 33.

15. See the sonnet to Anthony Cooke and Amour 28 (1594); Sonnets 2, 31, 46, (1599); Sonnet 66 (1602); Sonnet 47 and "To Sir Walter Aston" (1605); Ode "To Himself and the Harp" and "His Defense against the Idle Critic"; *Pastorals*, ecl. 5.

16. Stone, *Crisis of the Aristocracy*, p. 478.

17. *Historical Essays*, p. 181, and elsewhere.

18. Quoted in Stone, *Crisis of the Aristocracy*, p. 564.

19. It may be objected that I have not sufficiently explained Drayton's religious position to make any claims about his politics at this time. David Mathew notes that Warwickshire was a part of the country

where "bitterness against Rome was tempered by a daily intercourse with the adherents of the proscribed religion" (*The Jacobean Age*, p. 274), which may account for Drayton's "softness" on Catholicism at times (e.g., *Poly-Olbion* VI.301–4). However, I think Drayton gives an ample explanation of his views in the religious sequence of *The Owl* (ll. 899–918) where he shows, as we have seen, that none of the currently quarreling sects is truly religious.

20. On the possible literary enmity between Drayton and Hall, see *Works*, V, 25–26, 138 n. 5.

21. A partial basis for the discussion that follows is provided by Raymond Jenkins, "Drayton's Relation to the School of Donne," *PMLA*, 38 (1923), 557–87. See also *Works*, V, 207–8. Carew seems to have been a special target of those who opposed his courting of the Buckingham faction and the licentious direction of the "new" poetry that he represented. See Paul Delany, "Attacks on Carew in William Habington's Poems," *SCN*, 24 (1968), p. 36.

22. Perhaps this explains why Drayton is so often completely overlooked in anthologies of the seventeenth century, such as the much-used text by White, Wallerstein, and Quintana (New York: Macmillan, 1952), or the more recent one by Shawcross and Emma (Philadelphia: Lippincott, 1969).

23. L. A. Beaurline, "Dudley North's Criticism of Metaphysical Poetry," *HLQ*, 25 (1962), 299–313; Osborne quoted in George Williamson, "Strong Lines," *Seventeenth Century Contexts* (Chicago: Univ. of Chicago Press, 1961), p. 121; Drummond's letter to Arthur Johnston, Reynolds' *Mythomystes*, and North's criticism appear in *Literary Criticism of 17th Century England*, ed. Edward Tayler (New York: Alfred A. Knopf, 1967). Another opponent of strong lines was the Spenserian Francis Quarles, in his preface to *Argalus and Parthenia* (1629).

24. A distinction should also be made between this Spenserian tradition and what might be called the second-generation university Spenserians, like the Fletchers, Quarles, and perhaps the young Milton. The older group would seem to be attracted to Spenser's vatic nationalism; the second, to his intellectual eclecticism.

25. *Thalia's Banquet*, Epigram 38.

26. Edwin H. Miller, *The Professional Writer in Elizabethan England* (Cambridge, Mass.: Harvard Univ. Press, 1959), points out that "Since patrons rewarded reprints even less bountifully than new books, authors had to come into print much too frequently for their own good" (p. 129). Considering the number of carefully revised reprints Drayton published after 1600, we may admire both Dray-

ton's integrity and the generosity of Aston, who is his most consistent patron from 1600 on.

27. A similar observation is made on the new generation of dramatists in L. C. Knights, *Drama and Society in the Age of Jonson*, p. 261.

28. *An Apology for Poetry* in G. Gregory Smith, ed., *Elizabethan Critical Essays* (1904; rpt. London: Oxford University Press, 1964), I, 179–80.

29. *Works*, V, 291.

CHAPTER 6: ELYSIUM AND AFTER

1. Murray Roston, *Biblical Drama in England* (London: Faber, 1968), pp. 69–78.

2. Numerous other examples might be given of the appeal that this kind of scriptural interpretation had for devout seventeenth-century Englishmen. On his way to the Tower, Buckingham's assassin, John Felton, was applauded with shouts of "God bless thee, little David." The greatest literary products of this tradition come at the end of the century with *Samson Agonistes* and *Absalom and Achitophel*.

3. Robert R. Cawley, "Drayton and the Voyagers," *PMLA*, 38 (1923), 549, 555–56.

4. *Complaint and Reform in England*, eds. Dunham and Pargellis (New York, 1968), p. 482.

5. Introduction to *English Pastoral Poetry* (London: Harrap, 1952), p. 14.

6. *English Literature in the Sixteenth Century Excluding Drama* (New York, 1954), p. 535.

7. See Kermode, *English Pastoral Poetry*, p. 15. Jacobean satirical poets like Rankins and Wither often use pastoral motifs in this way.

8. *Works*, V, 220.

9. Newdigate, pp. 187–90.

10. Browne in *Works*, IV, 393. The author of "The Great Assizes" singles out for special praise the *Heroical Epistles, Legends*, and *The Battle of Agincourt*. See Luttrell Reprint, No. 6 (Oxford, 1948), p. 29.

11. H. R. Trevor-Roper, "The General Crisis of the Seventeenth Century," in *Religion, the Reformation and Social Change* (London: Macmillan, 1967), p. 88.

12. The tradition did not die easily. The public fields around Drayton's birthplace at Atherstone were not successfully enclosed until 1765.

See *A History of Warwick* (Victoria History of the Counties of England), IV (1947), 127.

13. Geoffrey Walton, "The Tone of Ben Jonson's Poetry," in *Metaphysical to Augustan* (London: Bowes and Bowes, 1955), rpt. in *Seventeenth Century English Poetry*, ed. William R. Keast (London: Oxford Univ. Press, 1971), p. 156.

14. *Sir John Oldcastle*, *Works*, I, 448. Cf. "The Library of Captain Cox," *The Gentleman's Magazine*, 180 (1846), 599–602.

15. This may explain his ambiguous status in the *PMLA* annual bibliographies. In the thirties and forties he was listed in the "Renaissance and Elizabethan" section; in 1957 he entered the "Seventeenth Century" section, only to fall back into the "Renaissance and Elizabethan" lists in 1967.

16. *Crisis of the Aristocracy*, p. 15.

17. Theophilus Cibber, *Lives of the Poets* (London, 1753), I, 218. Cibber's was not the only hand in this work, but the slur on Pope increases the likelihood that this passage is his.

18. Cf. James William Johnson, "What Was Neo-Classicism?" *Journal of British Studies*, 9 (1969), 49–70: "The Neo-Classical ideal was a complete correspondence between the public and private self in a society where public and personal benefit were identical, where the single man was a microcosm of the body politic. The moving cause of Neo-Classicism was to persuade men that self-love and social were the same, that ethics and civics were so akin as to provide the same rules for living the worthwhile life" (pp. 62–63). As here described, Neo-Classicism is anticipated by other Jacobeans like Daniel and Jonson. See also Johnson's *The Formations of English Neo-Classical Thought* (Princeton: Princeton University Press, 1967).

19. O. B. Hardison, *The Enduring Monument* (Chapel Hill: Univ. of North Carolina Press, 1962), p. 25.

20. Arthur B. Ferguson, *The Indian Summer of English Chivalry* (Durham, N.C.: Duke Univ. Press, 1960), pp. 142–81.

21. Max Rafferty, "Education for Patriotism in Our Schools," *Senior Scholastic* (Teacher's ed.), Feb. 4, 1965, pp. 10T, 12T.

APPENDIX B

1. "Drayton's Sirena," *PMLA*, 39 (1924), 816–36 (see pp. 830–32). "The Vision" is printed in *Works*, III, iii.

2. The relevant passages from *Conversations* are in Newdigate, pp. 136–37. Newdigate also believes Jonson's poem to be a burlesque.

3. Sidney, *An Apology for Poetry*, in Smith, *Elizabethan Critical Essays*, I, 156.
4. "Amongst whom, if I have praised, unfortunately, any one, that doth not deserve; or, if all answer not, in all numbers, the pictures I have made of them: I hope it will be forgiven me, that they are no ill pieces, though they be not like the persons." Dedication to *Epigrams* in *The Complete Poetry of Ben Jonson*, ed. William B. Hunter, Jr. (New York: Norton, 1968), p. 3.
5. *Apology for Poetry*, I, 159.
6. See "And must I sing?" published with *Love's Martyr* in 1601.

List of Works Cited

For a fairly complete bibliography of scholarship on Drayton, the reader is referred to Samuel A. Tannenbaum, *Michael Drayton (A Concise Bibliography)*, New York: Tannenbaum, 1941. This has been supplemented by George R. Guffey, *Elizabethan Bibliographies Supplements VII: Samuel Daniel 1952–1965, Michael Drayton 1941–1965, Sir Philip Sidney 1941–1965*, London: Nether Press, 1967. More recent scholarship may be found in the annual bibliographies of *PMLA* and the Modern Humanities Research Association.

CONTEMPORARY SOURCES

Anon. *Haec Vir: or The Womanish Man*. London, 1620.

———. *Hic Mulier or The Man-Woman*. London, 1620.

———. *Tom Tell-Troath*, in S. Pargellis and W. H. Dunham, eds. *Complaint and Reform in England*. 1938; rpt. New York: Octagon, 1968.

Breton, Nicholas. *The Court and the Country*. London, 1618.

Burton, Robert. *The Anatomy of Melancholy*, intro. Holbrook Jackson. Everyman's Library. 3 vols. London: Dent, 1968.

C., R. *An Old Thrift Newly Revived*. London, 1612.

Calendar of State Papers, Domestic, 1619–1623.

Campbell, Lily B., ed. *The Mirror for Magistrates*. 1938; rpt. New York: Barnes & Noble, 1960.

Chamberlain, John. *The Chamberlain Letters*, ed. E. M. Thomas. London: Murray, 1966.

Chapman, George. *Bussy D'Ambois*, ed. M. Evans. New Mermaids. London: E. Benn, 1965.

Clarendon, Edward Hyde, Earl of. *History of the Rebellion and the Civil Wars in England*. 7 vols. Oxford: Oxford Univ. Press, 1849.

Comes, Natalis. *Mythologiae*. Venice, 1581.

Drayton, Michael. *The Works of Michael Drayton*, eds. J. William Hebel, Kathleen Tillotson, B. H. Newdigate, and B. E. Juel-Jensen. 5 vols. Oxford: B. Blackwell, 1931–41; corrected ed., 1961.

————. *Michael Drayton*, ed. John Buxton. 2 vols. London: Muses' Library, 1953.

Fairholt, F. W., ed. *Poems and Songs Relating to George Villiers Duke of Buckingham.* Percy Society Reprint. London, 1850.

Fuller, Thomas. *The Worthies of England*, ed. John Freeman. London: G. Allen & Unwin, 1952.

Gray, Robert. *A Good Speed to Virginia.* London, 1609.

Hubert, Francis. *The Deplorable Life and Death of Edward the Second.* London, 1628.

Jonson, Ben. *The Complete Poetry of Ben Jonson*, ed. William B. Hunter, Jr. 1963; rpt., New York: Norton, 1968.

Osborne, Francis. *The Works of Francis Osborne, Esq.* 10th ed. London, 1701.

Peyton, Edward. *The Divine Catastrophe of the Kingly Family of the House of Stuarts.* 1652; rpt. London, 1731.

Pontano, Giovanni. *I dialoghi*, ed. C. Previtera. Florence: Sansoni, 1943.

Ralegh, Sir Walter. *History of the World*, in *Works of Sir Walter Ralegh, Kt.* 8 vols. 1829; rpt. New York: Burt Franklin, n.d.

Reynolds, John. *Votivae Angliae.* London, 1624.

Rich, Barnaby. *Faults, Faults, and Nothing Else but Faults.* London, 1606.

Rous, Francis. *The Oil of Scorpions.* London, 1624.

Sidney, Sir Philip. *Apology for Poetry*, in *Elizabethan Critical Essays*, ed. G. Gregory Smith. 2 vols. 1904; rpt. London: Oxford Univ. Press, 1964.

Smith, John. *A Description of New England*, in *Works*, ed. E. Arber. Westminster: A. Constable, 1895.

Spenser, Edmund. *The Complete Poetical Works of Spenser*, ed. R. E. Neil Dodge. Cambridge, Mass.: Riverside Press, 1936.

Standish, Arthur. *The Commons' Complaint.* London, 1612.

Stow, John. *The Annals of England.* London, 1592.

Tayler, Edward, ed. *Literary Criticism of Seventeenth-Century England.* Borzoi Anthology of 17th-Century English Literature. New York: Alfred A. Knopf, 1967.

Wilson, Thomas. *The State of England*, in *Camden Miscellany*, 16 (1936).

Wither, George (?). *The Great Assizes Holden in Parnassus.* Luttrell Reprint, No. 6. Oxford, 1948.

SECONDARY SOURCES

Anon. "The Library of Captain Cox." *The Gentleman's Magazine*, 180 (1846), 599–602.

Baker, Herschel. *The Race of Time*. Toronto: Univ. of Toronto Press, 1967.

Ball, Lewis F. "The Background of the Minor English Renaissance Epics." *ELH*, 1 (1934), 63–89.

Beaurline, L. A. "Dudley North's Criticism of Metaphysical Poetry." *HLQ*, 25 (1962), 299–313.

Berdan, J. M. "Marlowe's *Edward II*." *PQ*, 3 (1924), 197–207.

Blackburn, Thomas H. "Edmund Bolton's *The Cabanet Royal*: A Belated Reply to Sidney's *Apology for Poetry*." *Studies in the Renaissance*, 14 (1967), 159–71.

Buchloh, Paul-Gerhard. *Michael Drayton: Barde und Historiker, Politiker und Prophet. Eine Beitrag zur Behandlung der nationalen Frügeschichte Grossbritanniens in der englischen Dichtung der Spätrenaissance*. Kieler Beiträge zur Anglistik und Amerikanistik, Bd. 1. Neumünster: K. Wachholtz Verlag, 1964.

Bush, Douglas. *Mythology and the Renaissance Tradition in English Poetry*. 1932; rev. ed. New York: Norton, 1963.

Campbell, Lily B. "The Use of Historical Patterns in the Reign of Queen Elizabeth." *HLQ*, 1 (1938), 135–67.

Cawley, Robert R. "Drayton and the Voyagers." *PMLA*, 38 (1923), 530–56.

Charlton, Kenneth. "Liberal Education and the Inns of Court in the Sixteenth Century." *British Journal of Educational Studies*. 9 (1960–1), 25–38.

Cibber, Theophilus. *Lives of the Poets*. 2 vols. London, 1753.

Croce, Benedetto. *Ariosto, Shakespeare and Corneille*, trans. Douglas Ainslie. New York: H. Holt, 1920.

Cruickshank, C. G. *Elizabeth's Army*. 2nd ed. Oxford: Clarendon Press, 1966.

Davies, Godfrey. *The Early Stuarts, 1603–1660*. Oxford: Clarendon Press, 1937.

Davis, Walter R. " 'Fantastickly I Sing': Drayton's *Idea* of 1619." *SP*, 66 (1969), 204–16.

Dean, Leonard F. *Tudor Theories of History Writing*. Univ. of Michigan Contributions in Modern Philology, 1 (Ann Arbor, 1947).

Delany, Paul. "Attacks on Carew in William Habington's Poems." *SCN*, 24 (1968), p. 36.

Eliot, T. S. "Imperfect Critics," in *The Sacred Wood*. 1920; rpt. London: Methuen, 1964.

Esler, Anthony. *The Aspiring Mind of the Elizabethan Younger Generation*. Durham, N.C.: Duke Univ. Press, 1966.

Ferguson, Arthur B. *The Indian*

Summer of English Chivalry. Durham, N.C.: Duke Univ. Press, 1960.

Finkelpearl, Philip J. *John Marston of the Middle Temple.* Cambridge, Mass.: Harvard Univ. Press, 1969.

Fox, Levi, ed. *English Historical Scholarship in the Sixteenth and Seventeenth Centuries.* London: Oxford Univ. Press for the Dugdale Society, 1956.

Gagen, Jean. "Love and Honor in Dryden's Heroic Plays." *PMLA*, 77 (1962), 208–20.

Hardin, Richard F. "Convention and Design in Drayton's *Heroicall Epistles.*" *PMLA*, 83 (1968), 35–41.

Hardison, O. B. *The Enduring Monument.* Chapel Hill: Univ. of North Carolina Press, 1962.

Harriott, Rosemary. *Poetry and Criticism before Plato.* London: Methuen, 1969.

Harrison, Thomas P. "Drayton's Herbals." *Univ. of Texas Studies in English*, 23 (1943), 15–25.

———. *They Tell of Birds.* Austin: Univ. of Texas Press, 1956.

Heffner, Ray L., Jr. "Michael Drayton as a Pastoral Poet." Unpubl. diss. Yale Univ., 1953.

Jenkins, Raymond. "Drayton's Relation to the School of Donne as Revealed in 'The Shepherd's Sirena.'" *PMLA*, 38 (1923), 557–87.

Johnson, James William. "What Was Neo-Classicism?" *Journal of British Studies*, 9 (1969), 49–70.

Kermode, Frank. Introduction to *English Pastoral Poetry from the Beginnings to Marvell.* London: Harrap, 1952.

Knights, L. C. *Drama and Society in the Age of Jonson.* New York: G. W. Stewart, n. d.

———. "Shakespeare's Politics: with Some Reflections on the Nature of Tradition." *PBA*, 43 (1957), 115–19.

La Branche, Anthony. "Drayton's *Barons Warres* and the Rhetoric of Historical Poetry." *JEGP*, 62 (1963), 82–95.

Langbaum, Robert. *The Poetry of Experience.* 1957; rpt. New York: Norton, 1963.

Levy, F. J. *Tudor Historical Thought.* San Marino, Calif.: Huntington Library, 1967.

Lewis, C. S. *English Literature in the Sixteenth Century Excluding Drama.* London: Oxford Univ. Press, 1954.

Mathew, David. *The Jacobean Age.* London: Longmans, Green, 1938.

Miller, Edwin H. *The Professional Writer in Elizabethan England.* Cambridge, Mass.: Harvard Univ. Press, 1959.

Nearing, Homer, Jr. *English Historical Poetry, 1599–1641.* Philadelphia: n. publ., 1945.

Newdigate, B. H. *Michael Drayton and His Circle.* Oxford:

B. Blackwell, 1941; corr. ed. 1961.

Nietzsche, Friedrich. *Thoughts out of Season,* trans. A. M. Ludovici, in *The Complete Works of Friedrich Nietzsche,* ed. Oscar Levy. Vol. 5. 1909–11; rpt. New York: Russell & Russell, 1964.

Oruch, Jack B. "Topography in the Prose and Poetry of the English Renaissance, 1540–1640." Unpubl. diss. Indiana Univ., 1964.

Partridge, Eric. *Shakespeare's Bawdy.* 1947; rev. ed. London: Routledge & Kegan Paul, 1967.

Pearl, Valerie. *London and the Outbreak of the Puritan Revolution.* London: Oxford Univ. Press, 1961.

Penn, C. D. *The Navy under the Early Stuarts.* London: J. Hogg, 1920.

Praz, Mario. *Storia della letteratura inglese.* Florence: Sansoni, 1964.

Reese, Gertrude C. "The Question of Succession in Elizabethan Drama." *Univ. of Texas Studies in English,* 22 (1942), 59–85.

Rose, Mark. *Heroic Love: Studies in Sidney and Spenser.* Cambridge, Mass.: Harvard Univ. Press, 1968.

Roston, Murray. *Biblical Drama in England from the Middle Ages to the Present Day.* London: Faber, 1968.

Rowse, A. L. *The England of*

Elizabeth. New York: Macmillan, 1951.

Schönert, Jörg. "Drayton's Sonet-Revisionen." *Anglia,* 85 (1967), 161–83.

Smith, Hallett. *Elizabethan Poetry.* Cambridge, Mass.: Harvard Univ. Press, 1952.

Stone, Lawrence. *The Crisis of the Aristocracy.* London: Oxford Univ. Press, 1965.

Strong, Roy C. "The Popular Celebration of the Accession Day of Queen Elizabeth I." *JWCI,* 21 (1958), 86–103.

Taylor, Dick. "Drayton and the Countess of Bedford." *SP,* 49 (1952), 214–28.

Tillotson, Kathleen. "Drayton, Browne, and Wither." *TLS,* Nov. 27, 1937, p. 911.

———. "Michael Drayton as a 'Historian' in the 'Legend of Cromwell.'" *MLR,* 34 (1939), 186–200.

Tillyard, E. M. W. *Shakespeare's History Plays.* 1944; rpt. Harmondsworth: Penguin, 1964.

Trevelyan, G. M. *Illustrated English Social History.* Vol. 2. (*The Age of Shakespeare and the Stuart Period*). London: Longmans, Green, 1951.

Trevor-Roper, H. R. *Historical Essays.* 1957; rpt. New York: Harper Torchbooks, 1966.

———. *Religion, the Reformation and Social Change.* London: Macmillan, 1967.

Tuve, Rosemond. *Elizabethan and Metaphysical Imagery.* 1947;

rpt. Chicago: Univ. of Chicago Press, 1965.

Walton, Geoffrey. *Metaphysical to Augustan*. London: Bowes and Bowes, 1955.

Williamson, George. *Seventeenth Century Contexts*. Chicago: Univ. of Chicago Press, 1961.

Willson, D. H. *King James VI and I*. New York: Holt, 1956.

——. *The Privy Councillors in the House of Commons*. Minneapolis: Univ. of Minnesota Press, 1940.

Winters, Yvor. "The 16th Century Lyric in England." *Poetry*, 53 (1939), 258–72, 320–35; 54 (1939), 35–51.

Wright, Louis B. "Propaganda against James I's 'Appeasement' of Spain." *HLQ*, 6 (1943), 149–72.

Zagorin, Perez. "The Court and the Country." *EHR*, 77 (1962), 306–11.

——. *The Court and the Country*. New York: Atheneum, 1970.

Index